Y0-DBL-349

AN INTRODUCTION TO LINGUISTIC SCIENCE

BY

EDGAR H. STURTEVANT

Professor of Linguistics Emeritus in Yale University

NEW HAVEN

YALE UNIVERSITY PRESS

LONDON · GEOFFREY CUMBERLEGE · OXFORD UNIVERSITY PRESS

1947

Printed in the United States of America

PREFACE

This volume is intended for readers with no previous knowledge of linguistics; it is hoped that no one will have difficulty in reading and understanding all of it. This does not mean that scientific problems have been avoided, or that the content of linguistic science has been watered down. The guiding motto of the author has been the quotation from Thomas Huxley on the first page of the introductory chapter: "Science is . . . nothing but trained and organized common sense"; the language of our community, then, should be capable of conveying the science of our community to all its members. Technical terms have generally been avoided if the terminology of ordinary speech would do instead, and such technical terms as seemed necessary have been explained.

Obviously a book of this size is far from complete. It is hoped that most readers will go on to fuller discussions of the subject. By far the best book to follow this is Leonard Bloomfield's Language.[1] Other books will be referred to in the following pages.

All foreign words and forms are cited in transcription. Greek is written with Latin letters according to the system developed by the Romans, except that αι is written *ai;* ει, *ei;* οι, *oi;* ᾳ, *āi;* ῃ, *ēi;* ῳ, *ōi.* It should be noted that Greek κ is represented by *c,* and χ by *ch.* I have occasionally marked with a prefixed star a word that is not citable from any text, but I have not used this symbol before reconstructed forms that are clearly labeled as such in the context. The symbol > means "becomes" or "becoming," and < stands for "comes from" or "coming from."

Thanks are due to the many scholars who have contributed in one way or another to this book, especially to Leonard Bloomfield and Bernard Bloch of Yale and to Adelaide Hahn of Hunter College.

1. New York, Henry Holt and Co. (1933).

CONTENTS

PHONETIC SYMBOLS USED IN THIS BOOK

æ	Like *a* in English *cat.*
b	§ 18.
β	§ 20.
ç	Like *ch* in German *ich.*
č	§ 28.
d	§ 14.
ð	§ 14.
e	§ 21.
ɛ	§ 21.
ə	Like *a* in English *sofa.*
f	§§ 11, 20.
ϕ	§ 20.
g	§ 13.
γ	§ 13.
h	Like *h* in English *hat.*
ħ	§ 12.
ʿ	§§ 16, 18.
ɪ	§ 21.
j	Like *y* in English *yet.*
k	§ 13.
m	§ 13.
hm	§ 19.
m̩	§ 19.
ŋ	Like *n* in English *inḳ.*
n̩	Like *en* in English *fatten.*
o	§ 21.
ɔ	§ 21.
ϕ	§ 21.
p	§§ 16, 17.
pˇ	§ 17.
ʀ	§ 13.
s	§ 14.
š	§ 14.
t	§§ 14, 16.
θ	§ 14.
u	§ 21.
ʊ	§ 21.
ɯ	§ 19.
v	§§ 11, 20.
w	§ 20.
hw	§ 20.
x	§ 13.
y	§ 21.
z	§ 14.
ž	§ 14.
ʔ	§§ 11, 16.
·	§ 22. Indicates that the preceding character represents a long sound.
˛	e.g. [ą] Indicates that the character to which it is attached represents a nasalized sound, as *en* in French *cent.*

CHAPTER I

INTRODUCTORY

1. The English language, as everyone knows, has a double vocabulary; in addition to the words used in everyday life, we have another set of terms that tend to be used in books and public addresses, and also in conversation when the occasion is formal or when the subject-matter calls for precision. Since a large proportion of the words in this second vocabulary are loans from other languages, it has been called the **foreign-learned vocabulary.** It includes not only a great many learned-sounding synonyms for very plain words, such as *prestidigitation* for *sleight-of-hand* or *expectorate* for *spit,* but also most of our technical terminology.

2. An example of a foreign-learned term is the phrase *linguistic science* [1] in the title of this book. The word *linguistic* is merely the more formal and imposing synonym of the adjective *language;* in everyday speech one might as well say language science. Even that phrase, however, would have a special—a technical—sense, and so both words need further clarification.

Says Thomas Huxley, *Collected Essays,* 3.45: "Science is, I believe, nothing but trained and organized common sense." In other words, science is based upon the common man's tacit assumption that the evidence of the senses is valid. Of course the common man is always ready to revise his first interpretation of this evidence when he is compelled to do so. I once saw a man, walking along a hotel corridor, meet another man walking in the opposite direction. He bent his course a little to the right, but the other man turned left by an equal amount, and they would have collided if they had not both stopped short. Then the first man tried to pass on the left, but the second man moved to the right. Presently the man I had originally noticed revised his interpretation of the evidence: he was facing his own reflection in a mirror. So he walked off at a right angle to his original course. Just so science must frequently revise its conclusions, as when it became necessary to give up

1. A common variant for *linguistic science* is *the science of language.* More in harmony with the names of other sciences is *linguistics,* which implies the general term science as much as *physics* or *chemistry* does. We shall use the three terms interchangeably.

the naïve belief that the sun actually rises in the east and sets in the west. But after all it is the evidence of the senses upon which both the common man and the scientist base all their conclusions; for both, the philosopher's attempt to find a cogent theory of knowledge is irrelevant.

The common sense of one age differs from that of another; many of the obvious first conclusions of common sense have been permanently revised for all members of our community. None of our friends believe that the earth is flat and that the sun and moon move upward in the eastern sky and downward in the west.

The community of scientists devoted to a single subject is very much smaller than most social groups and it maintains accurate records of its observations and conclusions; each scientist is able to start where his predecessors left off. This is why the progress of science is so much more rapid than that of common sense. We may sum the matter up by saying that science is cumulative. A corollary is that a writer who neglects the work of his predecessors and contemporaries is wasting his time and the time of his readers; he has no right to call himself a scientist.

3. We shall have to examine the word *language* somewhat more carefully, since it indicates the branch of science that we are going to study. For our immediate purpose we may set up the following definition, and then consider several of the terms employed in it:

A language is a system of arbitrary vocal symbols by which members of a social group coöperate and interact.

The word *system* marks a language off from mere sets of nonsense syllables like *ta-ra-ra-boom-de-ay* or *a-heigh-and-a-ho-and-a-heigh-nonny-no.* With the proper rhythm and intonation these or any other groups of syllables can carry a highly emotional message, but they do not form a part of the systematic structure of the English language. In contrast the sentence *the dog bites the man* is thoroughly systematic; we can transpose the words *dog* and *man* and still be understood by all English-speaking hearers, although the meaning of the sentence *the man bites the dog* is absurd. In spite of an entirely different mechanism the two Latin sentences: *canis hominem mordet* and *homō canem mordet,* stand in a similar relative position; it is only the system of the Latin language that compels us to take the second sentence in a sense that defies all experience.

The key word of the phrase *arbitrary vocal symbols* is the noun *symbols.* A symbol necessarily involves a dualism; there must be something that stands for or represents something else. This may be indicated by a diagram:

$$\frac{\text{the signifier}^{2}}{\text{the signified}} \quad \text{or better} \quad \frac{\text{meaning}}{\text{form}}$$

In the case before us the *form* is any meaningful segment of an utterance, and the *meaning* is the meaning of that segment. An *arbitrary symbol* is one whose form has no necessary or natural connection with its meaning. English *dog* has roughly the same meaning as German *Hund,* French *chien,* Latin *canis,* and hundreds of other words in as many other languages. The only reason why *dog* carries this meaning is that the speakers of English use it with this meaning. The word *vocal* stands in the definition to exclude the human activities denoted by the phrases *gesture language, sign language, written language,* etc. All of these are important activities and proper subjects of investigation, and besides they have obvious connections with audible speech. The only reason for excluding them from our definition is convenience; they are found not to behave in the same way as audible language, and so they cannot conveniently be treated scientifically at the same time.[3]

The final clause of the definition—*by which the members of a social group coöperate and interact*—designates the chief function of language in society. There are, of course, other means of coöperation between living beings, as witness the wolf pack, the swarm of bees, etc. Even men may coöperate not only by writing or by gesture but by actual physical compulsion or by a smile or by the raising of an eyebrow. All we mean to say is that among men language is by far the commonest and most important means of coöperation. Society as now constituted could not long continue without the use of language.[4] We must not forget, however, that language may also be used to interfere with the action of a group or to oppose one group to another; we cannot end our definition with the word *coöperate.*

A corollary of the final clause of the definition is that a language cannot function normally unless there are at least two speakers of it. When only one speaker remains, the language may be said to be dead.

2. Cf. Ferdinand de Saussure, Cours de linguistique générale, Paris (1922). The horizontal line may be read, "combined with" or "simultaneous with."

3. We shall have to discuss writing in Chapter III and elsewhere, but only because writing embodies almost our only records of the speech of the past.

4. Cf. Bloomfield, Language, p. 24.

THE POSITION OF LINGUISTICS AMONG THE SCIENCES

4. *Physiology* and *Physics.* Since all speech sounds are produced by certain bodily organs and received by certain others, an important part of linguistics obviously belongs also to physiology. Both the action of these same organs in producing and receiving sounds and also the transmission of the sound waves from speaker to hearer fall within the sphere of physics. Those parts of linguistics that belong also to physiology or to physics are grouped under the term **phonetics.** Here linguistics is chiefly a learner; since their problems can be studied in simpler form elsewhere, physiologists and physicists are not likely to work with linguistic material.

5. *Psychology.* Any bit of human behavior may be designated as a person's reaction to his situation, where *situation* includes the total experience of the person and his physiological condition, as well as his surroundings at the moment. The situation and the reaction are connected by the person, who is affected by the one and performs the other. We may represent the entire process by this diagram,

situation → person → reaction

Psychology treats of the part of the process denoted here by the word person, namely, all that connects the situation with the reaction. There are two kinds of evidence available for this investigation.

(1). Each subject or person can report what seems to him to take place while the situation is leading to his reaction. Although no one else can directly check on his report, the psychologists have developed techniques for systematizing and standardizing such reports.

(2). It is possible to study quite objectively the situation and the reaction and their concomitant variations. Such study lends itself to laboratory experiment, and it can be checked in the same way as physical or chemical observation and experiment.

Either situation or reaction may consist in part of speech; if we disregard for the moment the residual factors, our diagram may become:

situation → person → speech
or: speech → person → reaction
or: speech → person → speech

Furthermore, the "person" sometimes reports that part of what happens within him between situation and reaction takes the form of speech; e.g., "When he hit me, I said to myself, 'nobody can do that to me and get away with it,' and then I hit him back." We may then modify our diagram thus:

situation → (internal) speech → reaction

Such talking to one's self, either aloud or silently, seems to accompany the solution of most, if not all, intricate problems, and it has long been held by many scholars that what we habitually call thinking is just this. It seems likely, however, that very simple or very familiar problems do not require the use of words. An experienced driver of an automobile can, in an emergency, apply his brakes or turn his steering wheel much more quickly than he can describe his operations. A hungry ape has been known to secure bananas hung above his head by putting one box on top of another and standing on top of the second; since the ape can do this without the aid of speech, we must conclude that a man can also do it without speech. Only more intricate problems are reasonably certain to make a man talk. I stand on the bank of a stream and I try to reach a floating object with a stick; if all the available sticks are too short, I may say to myself: "If I had a piece of string, I could tie two sticks together."

When it comes to such a problem as putting a plank over a stream, it is altogether likely that the use of language is essential. That is possibly just the reason why a man can do so many things that speechless animals have never been known to do.

It follows that linguistics and psychology are very close together and that the kind of experimentation that has done so much for psychology must be available also as a help on linguistic problems. We need scholars who are thoroughly at home in both fields.

6. In the meantime it seems wise for linguists not to subscribe to any of the schools which have hitherto divided the psychologists. George Lane has published [5] a brief account of how psychologic doctrines and doctrinaires have misled our science. Just possibly he might have included the American behaviorists with Herbart and Wundt; at any rate present-day psychologists seem to be less dogmatic mechanists than are certain linguists—including Lane himself! Nevertheless I heartily agree with Lane's conclusion, if I may delete one adjective and change another:

> It is a great relief to turn finally from the mass of psychological discussion prevailing at the turn of the century to the clear-cut statement of Bloomfield: "that we can pursue the study of language without reference to any

5. Studies in Philology, 42. 465–472 (1945).

one psychological doctrine, and that to do so safeguards our results and makes them more significant to workers in related fields" (Language, p. vii). When any one of the [mentalistic (*delete*)] systems of psychology becomes capable of demonstrating objectively that its particular theory of the operation of the mind is fact, then and only then, need the scientific linguist take it into account. It seems to me that we are far from that stage in the development of such systems. In the meantime the linguist will do well if he maintains a purely [mechanistic, *read:*] objective view of language.

7. *The Social Sciences.* Our definition of a language (§ 3) gives it a social function. A language can exist only in a social group, except that an isolated speaker of a language does not immediately forget it. And if the social group is necessary to the language, the language is quite as essential for the social group; since it is the one important set of signals from man to man, it does for the group what the nervous system does for the individual.

The use of a single language by widely separated groups of men implies the former existence of a single social group; the English of America, Australia, South Africa, etc., is explained by the migration of many speakers of the language from England. Just so a genetic relationship of a number of languages implies the former existence of a single language spoken by a single social group; the Romance languages imply the Roman nation, and the Indo-European languages imply the former existence of an Indo-European nation.

Linguistics is a social science, but it cannot be coördinated with the commonly recognized social sciences. These are primarily history, anthropology, and sociology. History is differentiated from the other two by its prevailing interest in the past. Sociology studies the present state of European and American Society, and anthropology the present state of other societies or cultures.[6] Most anthropologists include in their study of a particular culture more or less attention to the language of that culture, and some anthropologists are primarily interested in language. The sociologists do not pay much attention to languages, no doubt because other groups of scholars are at work upon the languages associated with European culture. Similarly the historians are interested in languages

6. The lines of division are not sharp; anthropologists treat of the history of a culture that has been neglected by historians. I leave out of account physical anthropology and also such subjects as economics and political science, since they have no close connection with linguistics.

only as tools, and in linguistics only as it furnishes evidence on prehistoric migrations. They leave the history of languages almost entirely to the linguists.

A logical division of social science would coördinate the science of language with the study of religion and mythology, the study of customs, and the study of government, each of these topics covering all mankind both in the present and in the past. Of course no such division is contemplated; and without it linguistics, as such, doesn't fit very well into the organization of the social sciences.

8. *Science in General.* All the sciences state their observations, problems, and conclusions in language; but this fact does not provide an additional bond between them and the science of language. Language is the one tool that man employs in nearly all his activities—in hunting, fishing, farming, and retail trade no less than in science and philosophy. All speech is raw material for the linguist, but that does not make the linguist a good farmer or storekeeper or physicist. Neither does it justify the claim of certain scholars that linguistics can make a noteworthy contribution to physics or to mathematics.

9. *Philology* [7] is a word with a wide range of meaning. I use it here to designate the study of written documents. The philologist devotes his attention first to establishing a correct text. He must often read and supplement more or less imperfect or mutilated inscriptions and manuscripts, and when he has several copies of a lost original he must determine the latter by comparing variant readings. Since all conclusions in this process must be checked against the possibilities provided by the language, he has to take account of linguistics at every step.

No less important is it to interpret the text when it has been established and to draw from it all possible information on history and culture, including language.

Since written documents contain all the information we have about the languages of the past, it is clear that all students of historical linguistics must deal with philology. It would be desirable for the linguist to deal fully with the philology of every text from which he cites even a single form, but for this he hasn't time. In accord with the usual division of scientific labor he must often rely upon the philological work of others. He must, however, be familiar with the methods and principles

7. See E. H. Sturtevant and Roland Kent, Classical Weekly, 22. 9–13 (1928); G. M. Bolling, Language, 5. 27–32 (1929); and references.

of philology, and he must know how to check his philological authorities in case of need.

This situation justifies the traditional close connection of historical linguistics with philology. Since the various stages of a language demand comparison, and since all languages, present or past, contribute to our generalizations about language, it would be inefficient to distribute the various aspects of linguistics among several departments.

In spite of the social importance of language, linguistic science must for the present continue to be grouped with the humanities.

CHAPTER II

PHONETICS AND PHONEMICS

10. The science of **phonetics** treats of the production, transmission, and reception of speech. It includes a description of the physiological mechanism of the lungs, throat, mouth, and nose, and also of the ear. A complete treatment of the subject would involve also an account of the nerves which control the production of sound, and of those which connect the ear with the brain. Equally essential is the physics of sound production and reception, and of the sound waves that pass from speaker to hearer. To handle the subject with any thoroughness, extensive laboratory equipment is necessary.

It is found in practice, however, that the laboratory phonetician spends only a relatively small part of his time on problems of direct concern to linguistics, and the linguist, on the other hand, cannot spare much time for laboratory work on phonetics if he is to get on with his study of other phases of language. Consequently a much abbreviated treatment of the subject from the point of view of general linguistics has been developed. The sole justification of this as of all other partitions of the field of science is the necessity for a division of labor. Practical phonetics as conducted by linguists confines itself to a description of the action of the organs of the throat and mouth in producing speech sounds.[1]

Even this is more than we can undertake to treat here; we have space for only a few specimen remarks, and we shall attempt to do just two things. First we shall identify the most important of the speech organs and give a few illustrations of what they can do. Then we shall give an account of the action of the lips in sufficient detail to suggest the infinite range of possible speech sounds.[2] We include in square brackets the symbols used in this book for each sound described.

1. It is not easy to draw a sharp line between sounds used in speech and other sounds made by the speech-organs. Therefore Kenneth L. Pike, Phonetics, a Critical Analysis of Phonetic Theory and a Technic for the Practical Description of Sounds, Ann Arbor (1943), includes all sounds produced in the throat, mouth, and nose.

2. For a much fuller but still brief treatment of phonetics see Bernard Bloch and George L. Trager, Outline of Linguistic Analysis, pp. 10–37, Baltimore (1942); see also references on pp. 80 f.

11. As the stream of air passes outward from the lungs, the first place where it can be checked is in the **larynx,** the box of cartilage at the top of the wind pipe, which is sometimes called the **Adam's apple.** This box contains two ridges or shelves of tissue running from back to front; they are called the **vocal cords,** and the space between them is called the **glottis.** When the vocal cords are brought together the glottis is closed and the stream of breath is completely stopped. If pressure from the lungs compresses the air behind the glottis and then the vocal cords are suddenly drawn apart, the result is a slight cough, which is known as a **glottal stop** [ʔ]. This sound is often heard in English; it serves for a ***t*** in certain words (e.g., *mountain*) in some American dialects, and it is well known in the Scotch pronunciation of *Saturday, bottle,* etc. If the vocal cords are drawn near together without complete closure of the glottis, the passage of the air sets their edges into rapid vibration, thereby causing the musical tone called voice; the chief difference between English [f] and [v] is that the latter is a voiced sound; if you place your hands over the ears and pronounce these two sounds, you will hear the buzz which accompanies the latter but not the former. If while the glottis is in this position, the vocal cords are stiffened to prevent vibration, the passage of the air produces a whisper. The glottis is fully open in the production of voiceless sounds like English [f].

12. As the air continues its journey, it comes next to the **pharynx,** the chamber between the tongue and the back wall of the throat. An incomplete closure of the passage may be produced here by retraction of the root of the tongue. Thus is produced Arabic voiceless [ħ].

13. At the top of the pharynx the stream of breath reaches the **soft palate** or **velum** (the back part of the roof of the mouth). An important function of the velum is to rise until it closes the passage between the mouth and the nose; this is its position while we swallow food and also during the utterance of a majority of the speech sounds. With the velum lowered so that the passage into the nose is opened, we pronounce the nasal consonants and all nasalized vowels and consonants. The chief difference between English [b] and [m] is that for the latter the nasal passage is open.

The **uvula** is the small flexible body that hangs from the back edge of the velum. If it is loosely cradled in a groove of the back surface of the tongue, the stream of air may set it in vibration; the result is the trilled uvular [R] of North German and of the French of certain provincial cities.

A closure between the back surface of the tongue and the velum produces English [k] and (voiced) [g]. There are many possible points in the velum for this closure and an equal number of possible varieties of [k] and of [g]. An incomplete closure in a similar position allows the air to pass with audible friction, producing the German *ch* in *ach* [x] or a corresponding voiced sound [γ].

14. An incomplete closure between the front surface of the tongue and the hard palate (the front part of the roof of the mouth) produces English [š] and [ž], as in *sure* and *azure.* With the tip of the tongue turned back and more or less approaching the hard palate one produces various types of American *r.*

The tip of the tongue may also articulate with various hard surfaces in front of the hard palate. With closure or partial closure against the **alveolar ridge** (just behind the roots of the upper teeth) one pronounces English [t, d, s, z]. The articulation of French [t, d] is further front, against the upper **teeth.** English *th* [θ, ð] may be produced with the tip of the tongue between the tips of the upper and lower teeth.

15. The easiest to observe of all speech organs are the **lips;** for this reason we select them for more extended treatment. We shall emphasize the variety of action of these organs in coöperation with the other speech organs already discussed. Although most of the sounds we are about to mention are often called **labials** or **labio-dentals,** not one of them could be produced by the lips or by the lips and teeth alone. All the speech sounds are produced while all the speech organs are in some position or other, and a complete account of any speech sound would have to record the position or the movement of each organ between lungs and lips.

16. A [p] between vowels is formed by closing the lips, impounding behind them breath under pressure from the lungs, and then suddenly parting the lips so as to release the impounded breath with a slight explosion. Like [t, k, ʔ], it is a member of the class of sounds called variously **stops** or **explosives.** There are several varieties of [p]. In English *pin* the explosion is followed by a vigorous puff of breath, but in English *spin* there is no such puff; in *pin* we have an aspirate [pʿ], but in *spin* a non-aspirate [p]. Most English speakers are unaware of this difference, but if one holds his hand before his mouth and pronounces the two words, he will feel the impact of the puff of breath as he speaks the former word. An equally clear demonstration is to reverse the direction of a phonograph record of the word *pin;* one hears something like [n·ɪhp]. In French and many other languages only a non-aspirate [p] is employed. In some languages [p] is formed, not with air under lung pressure, but with air compressed by raising the larynx; the glottis is closed and then the entire larynx lifted in such a way as to lessen the cubic contents of the mouth. Such a *p* is said to be **glottalized.** Many other voiceless consonants may be glottalized by a similar movement of the larynx, but at the moment we are considering only the labial sounds.

17. If *pin* is the first word in a sentence, the first step in its production may be omitted; the lips need not be brought together if they are already closed. If [m] precedes [p], as in English *ample,* the act of closure at the beginning of [p] is impossible; instead the velum is raised to close the passage to the nose. If English *dip* closes a sentence, the speaker need not open the lips at all; the explosion may be altogether omitted. In English *apt* the lips are not opened until the oral passage has been closed by the tongue against the alveolar ridge; there is no explosion for [p]. In the phrase *lamp mat,* the closure is made for the first [m] and is maintained for the second [m]; there is neither closure nor opening of the lips for [p], which therefore is marked solely by the release of breath through the nose when the second [m] begins.

While the lips are closed the back of the tongue may be pressed against the soft palate and then the entire tongue moved back so as to increase the cubic contents of the mouth. If then the closure of the lips is released, the result is a kiss. A somewhat similar sound, induced by lowering the larynx while the glottis is closed, is employed in certain languages of South Africa. This **labial click** may conveniently be written [pˇ].

18. French [b] differs from [p] in having musical tone or voice throughout. English [b], on the other hand, is usually only partly voiced; *but,* at the beginning of a sentence, starts with the glottis open and ends with closure enough to produce voice; while [b] in such a word as *ebb* at the end of a sentence has voice only in its first part. English [b] as well as [p] lacks one or more of its parts in certain positions; cf. *ambition, abdomen, amble.* In certain languages of India an aspirated *b* [bʿ] is heard.

19. A [b] pronounced with the nasal passage open becomes [m];

since no breath can be impounded in the mouth, there can be no explosion. A voiceless [hm] is occasionally used in some English words; regularly as the middle segment of the interjection *mhm.* A **syllabic** [m̩] is one which is the most resonant sound in its syllable, as in *rhythm* [rɪðm̩] or *bottom* [batm̩].

20. With the lips bunched and protruding more or less, we pronounce the **rounded labial spirants,** voiced [w] and voiceless [hw], of English *witch* and *twitch.*

With the lips in loose contact, so that breath escapes between them with a rubbing sound, one may pronounce **unrounded labial spirants,** either voiced [β] or voiceless [ϕ]. These sounds are not heard in English.

With the lower lip against the upper teeth we produce the **labiodental spirants,** voiced [v] and voiceless [f], of English *vine* and *fine.*

21. It is not customary to call any of the vowels labial, but the lips are more or less important in forming all of them. We shall mention only a few in which the lip action is easily observed.

With the lips rounded as for [w] and with the back of the tongue relatively near the soft palate, we pronounce English [u] of *fool.* With less rounding and slightly lowered tongue we pronounce English [ʊ] of *full.* With the tongue lowered a little more we produce English [o] of *pole.* With still less rounding and elevation of the tongue we get English [ɔ] of *all.*

These are by no means all the vowels that can be made with lip-rounding. French [u] of *poule* shows more rounding than any English vowel. There are many possible degrees of rounding and of tongue elevation between those employed in English. Then there is a series of vowels with rounded lips, but with elevation of the front of the tongue, French *u,* German *ü* [y], French *eu,* German *ö* [ø].

Instead of rounding the lips we may draw the corners of the mouth apart more or less—more in French, less in English. With the lips in this position and elevation of the front of the tongue, we pronounce English [i] in *keen,* [ɪ] in *pin,* [e] in *sale,* [ɛ] in *ten.* In addition there is a series of vowels without lip-rounding, but formed with elevation of the back of the tongue, e.g., Turkish *ı* [ɯ].

22. All of these vowels, and also [β, w, v], may be pronounced with the nasal passage open; they may be **nasalized,** and the degree of nasalization may vary from the full nasalization of certain French vowels to the nasal twang of some American dialects.

Any vowel or consonant may be made long by simply holding the articulation. A long vowel need involve no change in the character of its sound, however long it may be. A long stop, such as [p·], normally consists of the same three parts as any other [p], but it is only the central period, during which the breath is held behind the closed lips, that is lengthened, as in such a phrase as *top part.*

23. A variation of loudness within the limits of a single utterance is called **stress accent.** All languages present wide variations in loudness between different utterances, but some ordinarily show only slight differences in this respect between the parts of the same utterance. Such a language is French, which is said to have (relatively) level stress. English, on the other hand, sometimes distinguishes between otherwise identical words by means of stress accent; *increase* is a noun if the first syllable is the louder, but a verb if the second is the louder.

A variation of pitch within a single utterance is called **pitch accent,** and this term is sometimes applied to level pitch by contrast to neighboring parts of an utterance with rising or falling pitch. In Chinese, the pitch accent or the **tones,** to use the customary term of Chinese grammar, often distinguish between otherwise identical words. In Norwegian both stress accent and pitch accent help to distinguish between different words. English employs pitch accent, or **intonation,** solely in syntactic or stylistic function, as in these three sentences: *He is coming. He is coming? He is coming!*

24. The foregoing sketch is very incomplete, but it will suggest that the possibility of producing speech sounds is infinite. In fact, what limitation there is in this field is set by the ear; it can distinguish fewer sounds than the vocal organs can produce.

In the early days of linguistic science it was tacitly assumed that for grammatical purposes we could posit about as many speech sounds as are suggested by the Greek and Roman alphabets, except for differences between long and short vowels and consonants and some further details. As phonetic observation became more detailed and exact, scholars saw that they must recognize vastly more phonetic variation than they had supposed. The resulting complications made it more and more difficult to state problems in historical and comparative grammar, and some were inclined to despair of finding any solutions whatever. How could anyone make general statements about English *p,* if at each step he must distinguish between the [pᶜ] of *pin,* the [p] of *spin,* and the several partial *p's* discussed above (§ 17)? There was similar difficulty about *b,* which may be voiced for varying parts of its continuance, and which may be more or less complete (*about, ambition, blimp, amble*).

25. Some simplification was necessary if linguistic science was to continue; this has been provided by **phonemic analysis** or **phonemics.**[3]

There are in English no pairs of words distinguished solely by the fact that one contains [pᶜ] and the other contains [p]; there is always some other difference between the two members of the pair, such as the initial s of [spin] beside [pᶜin]. Native speakers of French, who have only [p] in their own language, are shocked by the aspiration of English [pᶜ], and speakers of Chinese, whose language marks differences of meaning by the presence or absence of aspiration, readily hear the difference between English [p] and [pᶜ]. The inability of most native speakers of English to hear this difference is a reflex of the fact that it never by itself marks a difference of meaning. All of this goes to show that the phonetic pair [p, pᶜ] constitutes a phonemic unit in English, although two similar sounds are phonemically as well as phonetically distinct in Chinese.

On the other hand there are many pairs of English words whose only mark of distinction is the contrast between [p, pᶜ] on the one hand and [b] on the other; e.g., *pin bin, cap cab, prim brim, played blade, ample amble, harper harbor, napping nabbing.* Consequently all native speakers of English hear the phonetic difference between [p] and [b], although it makes difficulty for native speakers of some other languages, as South German. English, then, has a phonemic as well as a phonetic distinction between [p] and [b].

Careful observation has shown that there are several phonemic differences between different local dialects of American English. Many, probably a majority, distinguish the vowels of *hoarse* and *horse, four* and *for, mourning* and *morning,* the first word in each pair having a closer *o* and the second a more open vowel [o]: [ɔ]. But some of the best known local dialects, including those of New York and Philadelphia, lack this distinction.[4]

A phoneme, then, is either a single speech sound or a group of similar

3. See Bloch-Trager, pp. 38–51, and references on p. 81.

4. Cf. Hans Kurath, Studies for William A. Read, pp. 166–173 (1940).

speech sounds, which in a given language function in the same way. As Bloomfield puts it, a phoneme is a minimum unit of distinctive sound-feature.

The numerous speech sounds observed by the phoneticians do actually exist in the several languages, but they fall into relatively few groups (not more than a few dozen for any one language) which we call **phonemes.** The several varieties of sound which make up a phoneme are known as **allophones;** in English the [pʻ] of *pin* and the [p] of *spin* are allophones of the phoneme *p*. Some allophones occur only in particular positions; English [pʻ] occurs only before an accented vowel and when not preceded by *s*. Free allophones are mere chance variations among the indefinite number of possible pronunciations of the phoneme.

26. All qualified scholars are agreed thus far on phonemics, and it is easy to persuade any intelligent speaker of English that the facts are as stated above.

Furthermore there is nothing new about phonemic analysis such as we have described, except that modern scholars have invented technical methods of performing the operation rapidly and accurately. At bottom the invention of an alphabet necessarily involves phonemic analysis. The alphabets of modern Europe are, of course, based directly or indirectly upon the Greek alphabet, and we cannot credit the men who initiated or developed them with any sort of phonemic analysis, except as to the points in which they departed from their models, and it is clear that even their innovations did not always reflect the phonemic facts. Nevertheless it can be no accident that several modern alphabetic systems (e.g., Spanish, Polish, Czech, Finnish, Hungarian) come reasonably near to the phonemic systems of the respective languages. More remarkable is the fact that precisely the earliest known alphabets are phonemically sound as far as they go. It is regrettable that the West Semitic syllabary **(§32. 4)** does not record the vowels, but no scholar doubts the essential accuracy, as far as it went, of its picture of the consonantal phonemes of early West Semitic speech. Similarly the Greek alphabet, in its several forms, reflects a good but incomplete phonemic classification, and we can trace several improvements in this respect which were developed within historic times. Alphabetic writing in India approached phonemic perfection more closely than it ever did in Greece, and again this cannot be an accident. We are forced to conclude that many men in various parts of the world have practiced essentially what we now call phonemic analysis.

That is precisely the reason why it was possible for the early linguists to utilize the linguistic records embodied in traditional alphabetic writing.

27. But I have hitherto described only a part of the activities of the students of phonemics, namely, the part in which they are all or nearly all in essential agreement with one another and with the best of their predecessors, to whom we owe alphabetic writing.

On the basis of such pairs of words as *kin keen, shin sheen, sin seen, grin green, grit greet, sit seat, pill peal, mill meal, bid bead, filled field,* etc., all must agree that English has a phonemic distinction which in these words is situated after the initial consonant or consonant group and before the final consonant or consonant group. Furthermore there is general agreement that the second phoneme of *kin, shin, sin, sit,* etc., is phonemically a unit. There is, however, considerable disagreement about the phonemic structure of the middle segment of *keen, sheen, seen, seat,* etc. Some are content to call it a single phoneme and to contrast it with the *i* of *kin* by writing *kin* [kɪn], but *keen* [kin]. Others find two phonemes in the central segment of *keen,* the vowel of *kin* and another phoneme, which they may identify with the initial consonant of *yet,* or which they may prefer to identify as vowel length; both groups write *kin* as [kin], while the former write *keen* as [kijn] and the latter as [ki·n]. This difference is tied up with various attempts to simplify the description of the language; in either case the vowel phoneme [ɪ] is eliminated at the expense of certain statements about diphthongs or about vowel length. It is quite certain that either of the two devices can be used to secure a net simplification of the description.

28. Another point of disagreement in English phonemics is the initial and final consonant or consonant group of such a word as *church.* Some prefer to write [č] and others [tš]. All are agreed upon the phonemic distinction between such pairs as *chunk junk, rich ridge;* the difference of opinion concerns the question whether *chunk* contains the initial consonant of *tin* followed by the initial consonant of *shin;* if it does, we can reduce the number of phonemes to be assumed for English.

29. It seems that such questions as these are on a different plane from the elementary phonemic analysis about which all modern scholars are agreed with one another and with the nameless makers of alphabets. The first task is to discover for each language just what phonemic distinctions are actively employed by the speakers of that language; apparently these are about the distinctions upon which scholars readily agree. Further

analysis and classification should of course be undertaken, and there is no doubt that such work has contributed to the advance of knowledge. We may reasonably hope for fuller agreement about this more abstract part of phonemics than is now apparent.

I have no technique for drawing the line between the two kinds of phonemics. Probably it is neither sharp nor fixed; certainly the observation that certain American dialects possess two separate vowel phonemes in English *can* [kæn] 'be able' and *can* [kæ·n] 'a container' resulted from a highly refined phonemic classification, but, once discovered, this distinction is as objective as the distinction between English [p] and [b].[5] My purpose here is to insist upon the importance and antiquity of objective phonemics, and upon the usefulness of more refined analyses and classifications provided they are recognized by all as tentative.

5. See George L. Trager, American Speech, 15. 255–258 (1940).

CHAPTER III

THE RELATION OF WRITING TO SPEECH

30. We have already noted (§§ 3, 7) that language constitutes the bond between the members of any social group, so that language alone makes organized society possible. Language is as ancient as human society.

By comparison, writing is a modern invention. If it seems to us to be very ancient, that is because history is recorded solely in writing, and so there can be no history more ancient than writing. The record of pre-history that can be constructed from archeological finds remains vague and colorless. In spite of its immensely long span, its record is so nearly empty of incident and of human interest that it appears brief. And not only is the origin of writing comparatively recent, its spread over the earth from its points of origin in Egypt, Mesopotamia, and China has for the most part occurred well within the historical period. Besides, the process is not yet complete; there are illiterate speakers of all languages, and perhaps a majority of the languages of the world have never yet been written by any of their native speakers.

That there is a close relationship between specific languages and specific systems of writing is obvious; an English book can be read only in the English language, and a Chinese book only in a Chinese language. To be sure, there is not always a one-to-one correspondence; there are several mutually unintelligible Chinese dialects, and a given book can be read by an educated speaker of any one of them. In general, however, the intimate connection of writing and speech is clear; it follows, therefore, from the greater antiquity of speech, that writing must be only a more or less close representation of speech.

31. That is not to say, of course, that communication necessarily depends upon speech. Lynd Ward [1] has shown that a story can be effectively told by pictures, with only slight use of titles. The silent movies generally made liberal use of titles, but even so the pictures carried most of the message.

1. God's Man, a Novel in Woodcuts, New York (1929); Madman's Drum, New York (1930), and several other books.

The picture writing of the American Indians had to depend entirely upon familiarity with the practice of communication by this means, and a knowledge of the subject of the particular message. Since there was no connection with any one language, speakers of different languages could understand the message.

Figure 1 is a reproduction of a letter from an Indian chief to the president of the United States, the original of which is in colors.[2] Numerals are here inserted for the purpose of reference. The recipient of the letter (8) has a white face and stands in a white house: "to the white

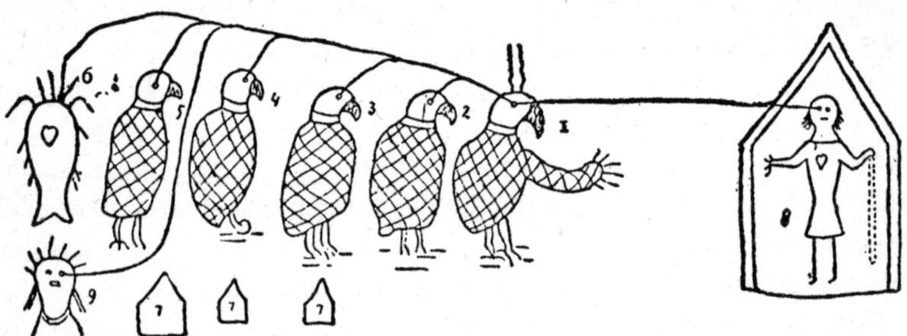

Figure 1.

man in the White House." The writer (1) belongs to the eagle totem; the lines rising from his head indicate that he is a chief; his extended arm denotes an offer of friendship. Behind him stand four warriors of the eagle totem. No. 6 is a warrior of the catfish totem. No. 9 is not identified by his totem, but the larger number of lines rising from his head indicate that he is a more powerful chief than No. 1. The lines connecting the eyes indicate harmony. The houses under three of the warriors indicate that they will adopt white men's customs. The letter may be read more or less as follows: "I, a chief of the eagle totem, several of my warriors, who belong to the eagle totem, another of the catfish totem, and a certain chief who is more powerful than I are assembled and offer our friendship to you, the white man in the White House. We hold the same views with you. Three of my warriors will live in houses." Of course these words are far more explicit than the picture at several points, and, by the same token, the picture can quite as well be interpreted by several other sequences of words—in English or in any other language.

2. Reproduction and (in the main) interpretation are from Henry R. Schoolcraft, Historical and Statistical Information Respecting the Indian Tribes of the United States, 1. 418 f.

32. We have no record of the development of picture messages into a record of actual speech, and we have only fragmentary hints of the further development into alphabetic writing; but wherever such development has been spontaneous we may safely assume the following five processes.

32.1. The pictures were simplified and conventionalized as in such Egyptian hieroglyphs as [eye] 'eye,' ⊙ 'sun,' [front] 'front,' [face] 'face,' [go] 'go,' or in Chinese 人 'man,' or in Sumerian [hand] 'hand.' As development in the same direction continued the original picture often became quite unrecognizable, as in later Sumerian [hand] 'hand.'

32.2. Prior to our earliest records of writing many signs had gained a phonetic value like the picture syllables in a rebus, e.g., [cap] [tain] 'captain,' [man] [date] 'mandate.' Thus Egyptian [face] represents primarily the word *hr* (perhaps [her]) 'face' and also the same combination of consonants [hr, her, here, hre, har] etc., in any other word. (In Egyptian writing the vowels were left unrecorded.)

32.3. Then the sign might be used to represent only a part of the phonetic value of the word. Thus in Egyptian the picture of a mouth may stand for *rʔ* (= [reʔ] [3]) 'mouth' or just for the sound *r*, either alone or followed by any vowel. Such a uniconsonantal sign existed for every one of the twenty-four Egyptian consonants, and it would have been possible to write the language by means of them alone. The Egyptians, however, never gave up their pictures or their phonetic signs representing groups of consonants.

32.4. There is no such similarity between Egyptian hieroglyphs and the letters of any West Semitic alphabet that has been preserved as to prove that one is the source of the other. Nevertheless it can scarcely be an accident that the systematic structure of the West Semitic alphabets is precisely what would have resulted if the Egyptians had given up their word signs and their signs for two or more consonants; in their earliest forms the Semitic alphabets represent each consonant by a separate letter, and leave the vowels quite unrecorded. There may have been an intermediary between Egyptian and West Semitic writing (e.g., the still uninterpreted linear script of ancient Crete), but the ultimate derivation of the latter from the former is certain. The simplification

3. The word contained some vowel, but which one is not known.

of the system made by the Semitic scribes or their predecessors was of first-rate importance. It is customary to speak of the Egyptian uniconsonantal signs as alphabetic, and one hears constantly of the North Semitic or Phoenician or Arabic alphabet. Strictly all of these are rather syllabic scripts; [4] each character stands for a consonant and the following vowel, unless, to be sure, it forms the first member of a consonant group.

32. 5. The final stage in the development of our alphabet was the writing of vowels. It occupied several centuries.

Some time after the introduction of the Semitic syllabary certain consonants were lost in certain Northwest Semitic languages, but, with the usual conservatism of spelling, the signs for these consonants continued to be written. Thus the loss of final *h* sometimes left *ō* as the final sound of a word; hence the written *h* was reinterpreted as a mark of this vowel. Similarly when *aw* and *uw* became *ō* and *ū*, the *w* automatically became a sign of those long vowels; and the parallel development of *ay* and *iy* to *ē* and *ī* gave the written *y* the value of these long vowels. Such syllabic signs with secondary vocalic value (commonly called *matres lectionis* by medieval and modern scholars) had only a limited development in ancient Semitic writing.[5] Not before the fifth or sixth century A.D. do we find a system of vowel points, such as appear in modern Arabic and Hebrew books.

Long before this, Greek borrowers of the syllabary took the final crucial step to an alphabetic system. Since Greek *iota* clearly comes from Old Semitic *yodh,* one may suspect that its use as a vowel sign was taken directly from some Semitic document in which the character was used as *mater lectionis* in the value of a long *ī*. The case may be parallel with Υ from Semitic *waw,* although this Semitic character survives also in dialectic Greek ϝ with the value of [w].[6]

4. See Holger Pedersen, Linguistic Science in the Nineteenth Century, pp. 180–182, Cambridge (1931).

5. Hans Jensen, Die Schrift in Vergangenheit und Gegenwart, pp. 209 f., Gluckstadt and Hamburg (1935).

6. If it can be shown that the Greeks borrowed the syllabary before the changes *ay* > *ē*, *iy* > *ī*, *aw* > *ō*, *uw* > *ū* in the Semitic language concerned, we shall have to assume that the use of the characters as vowels developed independently in Greek. In any case the use of Ι and Υ as second member of a diphthong must go back to the earliest writing of Greek; perhaps οἶκος (*oicos*) was written ΙΚΣ. Similarly we may assume that the consonantal glide between ι and a following vowel was written (as it is in the Cyprian syllabary, where we read *i-ya-sa-ta-i* for *iyasthai*), so that *iatrós* may at first have been written ΙΤΡΣ.

Since Greek had no glottal stop the name of the letter *ʔalef* was borrowed with an initial vowel as Greek *alpha,* and the initial phoneme of the name became the value of the letter. Just so early Greek probably did not have [h] as a separate phoneme;[7] therefore the name *hē* for the letter ꟻ became *ē* (written ει in early Greek) and its value was *e* (long or short). (The familiar name *epsilon* 'mere *e*' is a late invention to point the contrast between ε and ει, when these were corresponding short and long.)

33. It must be admitted that we have no contemporary evidence for any of the developments outlined in the last two paragraphs, but they gain plausibility from the known history of the letter H from Semitic *cheth.*

In the early inscriptions of most Greek dialects, including Attic, H has the value [h]. In eastern Ionic and in the earliest inscriptions of Crete H is a vowel. Besides, it must occasionally, in various early inscriptions, be read as a sign for consonant plus vowel (HKHBOΛOI = *Hecēbolōi,* HPA = *Hērā,* HPMAIOΣ = *Hermaios,* etc.). The consonantal value and the syllabic value had their direct prototypes in Semitic usage, except that the Greek consonant was no longer, in historic times, a strong spirant; it was [h] rather than [x]. The use as a vowel developed in east Ionia and elsewhere upon the loss of [h]; this changed the name of the letter from *hēta* to *ēta,* and its value from [h] to [ɛ·]. In eastern Ionic there were two long *e*-vowels, close *ē* [e·] from earlier [e + e] or lengthened [e], and open *ē* [ɛ·] from earlier [ɛ·] or [a·]; the new vowel letter was used for [ɛ·], while [e·] continued to be written E. Eastern Ionic also had two long *o*-vowels, [o·] from earlier [o + o, e + o, o + e] or from lengthened [o] and open *o* [ɔ·], inherited from Proto-Indo-European[8] *ō*. On the analogy of H beside E, a variant form of the letter O, namely Ω, was utilized for [ɔ·].

34. For the Greek alphabet, from which our own is derived, we can be certain of the above five stages of development out of picture writing pure and simple; we cannot clearly document the early stages, and

7. If Greek had possessed the rough breathing (i.e., aspiration) at the time when the alphabet was borrowed, Semitic *hē* would have carried that value. We are forced to conclude that the change of *s* to *h* in such words as *hēmi-* 'half' (Latin *sēmi-*) had at that time reached the stage [x], and hence it was at first written by the Semitic letter *cheth.*

8. Proto-Indo-European is the reconstructed ancestor of the Indo-European languages, of which Greek is one (§ **224–6**).

several of the stages no doubt overlapped, but they all occurred, and in about this order. First the pictures were conventionalized and simplified. Secondly they gained conventional phonetic values. Thirdly some of the signs came to stand for a single consonant each, although most of them continued to be used for whole words or segments of words. Fourthly all machinery aside from the uniconsonantal signs was abandoned. Fifthly vowel letters came to be written.

35. Traces of these five steps in the development of alphabetic writing, or some of them, can be observed in many parts of the world. It appears that everywhere the chief improvements come at the time when a system of writing is utilized for a new language. The reason is that writing, an art that has to be learned from a teacher, is everywhere highly conservative.

Since the same situation blocks spelling reform among us, we may illustrate with English examples. If a man has been taught to spell *sight* and *white* he will object to a simplification of the system that would require him to spell the first word *site;* he will almost certainly dig up an absurd reason for not doing so: "The reader might confuse 'vision' with 'situation'!" It is only when the application of the system to a new language is required that the intelligence of the user has a chance. Hence word-signs and the like were retained in Egyptian but were not carried over into Semitic; and the consistent writing of vowels had to await the transfer of Semitic writing to Greece and to India.

36. The ideal alphabet would have one letter and only one for each phoneme or speech sound; but no alphabet in common use has ever reached this goal. A number of European alphabets come near enough to it so that children, once they learn to write, need not waste any appreciable further time in learning to spell. Spanish orthography, for example, is excellent, but even here [ka] is written *ca* and [ki] is written *qui,* while *ci* denotes an entirely different consonant plus vowel, [θi] in Castile, [si] in America. And here we come upon an insuperable difficulty; since all the great languages of civilization are split into dialects, it is necessary either to write each dialect in its peculiar form or to write some of them inexactly. In American Spanish it would be convenient to write the verb *citar* 'make an appointment, convoke' with an initial *s,* but that would not do at all for Castilian. And if such a reform should be adopted in America, a serious obstacle to the use of a given book

throughout the Spanish-speaking world would be set up; for example, it would be somewhat difficult for speakers of American Spanish to find the verb *sitar* in a dictionary published in Spain. Apparently a perfect alphabet is quite beyond the range of possibility.

37. There is no doubt, however, that most European languages are far worse off than need be. Since all languages constantly change, the conservatism of writers tends to make the correspondence of writing to speech ever less exact. Only a succession of spelling reforms could keep the two in even approximate agreement. Besides, misplaced learning has foisted upon us such monstrous spellings as English *doubt* for a word borrowed from French *douter,* although the *b* of Latin *dubitō* was lost before the earliest records of Old French. Just so, irrelevant scholarship has given us an *s* in *island* from Old English *īegland,* because of the *s* in Latin *insula.* Similarly French *poids* 'weight' gets a *d* from Latin *pondus* 'weight,' although the word itself comes from Latin *pēnsum* 'something weighed, weight.'

When natural conservatism and scholars' delight in Latin spellings are fortified by formal training of the young in a traditional orthography, all the inherited faults of the system are held fast and all those that arise from time to time are promptly incorporated.

Hence it comes that French has seven ways of writing [są], thirty for [o], fifty-two for [ą̧], fifty-five for [ɛ]. It is doubtful whether any more excess machinery can be claimed for English, but we are worse off than the French, since we have far more utterly erratic spellings that cannot be brought under any rule. It would scarcely be possible to cite from French such an utterly bewildering phrase as *though the tough cough and hiccough plough me through.*

Several times within the last century efforts have been made to eliminate some of the worst features of English spelling, and once the movement was promoted by an imposing organization of scholars equipped with financial support, namely, the Simplified Spelling Board. The results attained have been negligible, and hardly anyone now seems to have hopes of improvement in English spelling. It may perhaps be suggested that the most efficient as well as the easiest way to improve the situation would be the complete cessation of the teaching of spelling. This would shorten the school course by a year or two, adding that much to the useful life of every child, and saving considerable sums of money now wasted. But of course there are several vested interests, which may be counted on to prevent that reform.

38. Bad as English spelling is, we have not lost all or even most of the advantages of alphabetic writing. If we must spend, on the average, a year or two in learning to spell, the Chinese must devote many years to learning characters if they are to have complete command of the literature. One result is, of course, the wide prevalence in China of complete or partial illiteracy; the chances are that the laundryman who writes more or less beautiful characters on his tickets cannot do much in the way of reading books. Another result is that even the young Chinese who attend our graduate schools have spent so much time on the characters that they are far behind Americans of their age in other kinds of learning. It is safe to say that the Chinese, in spite of their high intelligence, must adopt an alphabet before they can rival Europeans or Americans in science, engineering, or scholarship in general.

39. We have seen that writing originated much later than language and that its development out of pictures has consisted, in large part, of a gradual approximation to speech; at first the pictures represented the material world directly, but they came, in the process of time, to stand for the forms of a language and to picture these more and more accurately.

40. The genetic relationship of systems of writing is independent of linguistic relationship. Chinese writing is used, with certain modifications, by the Japanese, but the Japanese language is quite unrelated to Chinese. **Cuneiform writing**[9] was passed over from Sumerian to the totally unrelated Akkadian, the Semitic language of ancient Mesopotamia; and some centuries later it was borrowed from Akkadian by the non-Semitic Hurrians whose ethnic center lay to the north of Mesopotamia, about Lake Van. From the Hurrians, probably, the cuneiform system was taken over for writing Hittite, which was related neither to Sumerian, nor to Akkadian, nor to Hurrian.

We have noticed that the West Semitic syllabary was adapted from Egyptian writing. It was passed on to other Semitic languages, Arabic, South Arabic, and Aramaic, and also to Greek, a non-Semitic language. The Arabic syllabary came to be used for numerous languages whose

9. Wedge-shaped characters constituting a syllabary widely used in the ancient Near East. Some of the characters are reproduced in § 45.

speakers embraced Islam, e.g., Turkish, Persian, Malay, and the Berber languages of North Africa, which represent four distinct linguistic families. The Aramaic syllabary gave rise to the two Indic scripts, and these have been and are still used for languages of the most various families throughout central and southeastern Asia, e.g., Sanskrit and its medieval and modern descendants, several Dravidian languages, Tibetan, Thai, Burmese, Javanese, etc. From the Greek alphabet are derived the Phrygian, Lycian, Lydian, and Etruscan alphabets, but one of which was employed for an Indo-European language. At a later date the Greek alphabet gave rise to the early Germanic runes, and later still to the various Slavic alphabets. From Etruscan came the various early Italic alphabets, including the Latin alphabet.

Although writing is completely unlike language in origin, history, and distribution, and although relatively few of the generalizations that can be established about language are true also of writing, it is impossible for linguists to neglect the study of writing. Except for the few years since the invention of the phonograph, we have no record of any language of the past except in writing.[10]

41. But since linguistic science deals only with speech (§ 3), the linguist cannot analyze written records until he has given them a phonetic interpretation. For some of the best known languages of the past this can be done with considerable certainty, although we cannot hope to secure anything like the accurate detail that we can observe in languages still spoken. For Sanskrit we have descriptions of articulation about as clear as those written by modern phoneticians. For the more recent stages of modern European languages we can secure very satisfactory results by checking the present-day pronunciation against rimes, variations in spelling, and old pronouncing dictionaries.[11]

42. We can reconstruct the pronunciation of other languages of the past only by assembling scraps of evidence from various sources. An illustration of the method is the evidence which shows that Latin *c* represents a velar stop [k] before *e* and *i* as well as in other positions.[12] Since most of the Romance languages show an altered pronunciation of *c* before front vowels (Rumanian and Italian [č], French and Portu-

10. Perhaps an exception should be made of a few ancient texts that were long handed down purely by oral tradition, notably the Hindu Vedas.

11. See Jespersen, A Modern English Grammar, 1. 1–13 (1909).

12. See Sturtevant, The Pronunciation of Greek and Latin 2d ed. pp. 165–169 (1940).

guese [s], Castilian Spanish [θ]) many scholars have assumed that the alteration began in classical times or earlier. Aside from the troublesome question whether Italian [č] or Old French [ts] should be assumed for Latin, two Romance languages, central Sardinian and the recently extinct Dalmatian, retain [k] before front vowels (e.g., Sardinian *kentu*, Dalmatian *kerkellu*). If Latin [k] before front vowels became [č] or [ts] in ancient times the change did not extend to Sardinia and Dalmatia. It cannot be said that the Romance evidence as a whole favors any considerable difference in the sound of Latin *c* before *e* and *i*.

Donatus, who lived in the fourth century, says: "*k* and *q* seem superfluous to certain writers, who do not know that whenever *a* follows, *k* should precede, not *c*, and whenever *u* follows, we should write *q*, not *c*." Donatus does not say that *c* had only one value, but he seems to assume just that. It is only fair, however, to remember that he is reproducing traditional material; perhaps it is only Donatus' authorities who knew of only one value for *c*.

The Latin inscriptions show *k* not only before *a* as in *K.* = *Caeso* and *Kal.* = *calendae* but also before front vowels in such forms as *Keri*, *Dekem*(*bres*), *Mukianus*, *Markellino*, *pake*. In harmony with this is the regular equation of Greek κ and Latin *c* in loan words, e.g., καλανδαι, κομετιον, Κικερων, Μαρκος, *Calacte* (καλὴ ᾿Ακτή), *colossus*, *Cepheus*, *cithara*, *Cynicus*. This system shows no sign of breaking down until after classical times.

Other languages also show loan words with *c* before *e* or *i* in the value of [k]. An example is Gothic *lukarn* 'lamp' from *lucerna*. German *Kiste* 'chest' from *cista* and *Keller* 'cellar' from *cellārium* must have been borrowed earlier than such words as *Zeder* 'cedar' from *cedros* and *Zirkel* 'circle' from *circulus*.

In Cicero's time many Romans spoke Greek, and they undertook to pronounce Greek loan words accurately even when speaking Latin. Consequently they pronounced [pʻ, tʻ, kʻ] in such words as *Philippus*, *Thēbae*, and *chlamys*. This pronunciation came to be a mark of aristocratic standing, and climbers, such as Arrius in Catullus, 84, tried to use it and frequently introduced it into genuine Latin words like *chommoda* for *commoda*. Cicero, Orator, 160, gives us a list of Latin words in which he had himself come to use aspirated stops so as not to be conspicuous. One of these words is *pulcher*, and he implies that he had heard *Orchivius*. Quintilian, 1. 5. 20, records also *chenturio*. Since all the other examples cited by the two authors in these sections contain *h* after a stop sound, and since the feature under discussion arose in imitation of Greek ϕ, θ, and χ, we must assume that in Cicero's time *c* before *e* and *i* was a stop.

After examining these various scraps of evidence no one can escape the conclusion that Latin *c* represented a stop before *e* and *i* as well as in other positions. More or less similar evidence establishes within certain limits the value of each letter of the Latin alphabet in classical times, and also of each letter of the Greek alphabet as employed in the dialects most abundantly attested by the documents.

43. For many ancient languages evidence is much less abundant, but we are not completely in the dark about any language whose texts we can understand.

CHAPTER IV

RECORDS OF SPEECH

44. A botanist or a zoologist can go for a walk almost anywhere and bring back specimens that will reward study. A linguist can easily find raw material for his study, but he cannot so easily bring it home or preserve it. Language consists of acts of certain human organs and of sound waves in the air; it is as concrete as the plants and animals, but each specimen exists only a moment. A linguist who is studying his native language can produce part of his needed material at will; and if working on a living language, he can base his study upon actual speech, and he can often induce other men to give him the very item he needs at the moment. But study involves fixing the attention upon a given material for some time. Linguistic material can be studied only as long as the linguist remembers it, unless he has some sort of record.

This is one reason why most linguistic study of the past has been based upon texts; imperfectly as traditional writing records speech, it has the immense advantage of relative permanence. With its aid the linguist can study languages that ceased to be spoken long ago; written documents do for the linguist what fossils do for the biologist.

45. In conducting these studies linguists are powerfully assisted by various systems of transcribing unfamiliar kinds of writing in Latin letters. There is, for example, a generally recognized transcription of the cuneiform syllabary (§ 40 and n. 9) which utilizes accents and subnumerals to distinguish homonymous signs, so that a competent scholar can restore the original text,[1] e.g.,

= *a*, = *á*, = *à*, = a_4, = a_5;
= *aš*, = *áš*, = *àš*, = as_4; = *be*,
= *bé*, = *bè*, = be_4.

1. See F. Thureau-Dangin, Le syllabaire accadien, Paris (1926), and Les homophones sumériens, Paris (1929).

It is cheaper to print anything but solid text with this transcription than with the cuneiform characters themselves, and it forms a very useful first step in interpretation; but the system is itself very awkward and difficult. It has to be supplemented by an approximately phonemic writing, which is readily deduced from it by omitting hyphens and extra vowel-signs; *ú-ul* means *ul* 'not,' and *ir-ti*$_4$*-i-ḳi* implies *irtiḳi* 'your breast' (genitive).

46. If the native alphabet is already phonemic or nearly so, representation by Latin letters is fairly easy, although disagreement among scholars may complicate the matter. An excellent system of printing Sanskrit in Latin letters has been pretty well agreed upon, except that some prefer *ç* and others *ś* for the palatal sibilant (perhaps similar to the German *ich*-sound; perhaps like Russian palatalized *s*).

It would be easy to print Hebrew, Arabic, and Greek in Roman letters, and such a practice would greatly reduce the cost of bookmaking. It would also appreciably lighten the load of beginners in those languages. Words cited in English books had better be printed in Latin letters if they are to be intelligible to all readers; that practice is followed in this book. The objections urged by scholars to the use of the Latin alphabet for writing and printing Hebrew, Arabic, and Greek are similar to the reasons why men cling to the absurd orthography of French and English and prefer the English weights and measures to the simplicity of the metric system.

47. By means of writing, again, a linguist can record a word, a sentence, or a bit of conversation and study it at his leisure; within certain limits writing makes possible linguistic collections more or less analogous to the collections in museums upon which systematic biology is largely based, and to the smaller collections that the individual biologist uses alongside of his experimental work.

Of considerable use in making and publishing such collections is the device of **phonetic writing.** We have seen **(§ 36)** that a phonemic alphabet is the most efficient way of writing any language; but it is often necessary to discuss the phonetic nature of a phonemic system. Furthermore, one can start recording a new language only by observing as many phonetic differences as he can in the speech of his informant. For such purposes scholars have gradually reached a partial agreement on the phonetic values to be assigned to certain signs; illustrations of phonetic symbols have been given in square brackets in §§ 11–22 above. The most widely used phonetic alphabet is that of the International Phonetic Association [2] (abbreviated IPA).

48. There are two large groups of linguistic facts that have until recently largely remained unrecorded. I refer to **local dialects** and to **lapses.** The former have been studied with constantly increasing energy for the last seventy years, and they have contributed a great deal to our understanding of linguistics. Lapses have been studied by only two or three scholars and what they can contribute to the science remains for the future to show.

DIALECT GEOGRAPHY

49. Local varieties of speech have always been noticed; we find references to them in all literary remains that contain comments of any extent upon contemporary speech. In the Indic drama several different dialects are assigned to the characters according to their social position; the distribution has no observable connection with geography. Just so the normalized Doric in the choral odes of Greek tragedy, interrupting the Attic of the dialogue, is employed in the same way whatever the nationality of the chorus is supposed to be. Aristophanes, on the other hand, introduces, in the Lysistrata, a number of Spartans speaking local dialect that is, in part, quite genuine.

In modern novels the use of dialect is a favorite means of securing local color, but such material is far too inaccurate to be used for scientific purposes.[3] Even the authors who have claimed to give genuine representations of local speech have in general got their effects by making their characters use non-literary forms that might be heard anywhere (*seen* = *saw, huntin* = *hunting, betwix* = *between, git* = *get, ḳem* = *come, gal* = *girl, fer* = *for, heerd* = *heard, you was*), seasoned by a few forms that belong more or less clearly to the region depicted. As a rule, little or no effort is made to tell the reader how he should interpret the dialect spellings employed; if anyone interprets Joel Chandler Harris' *Brer* (*Brer Rabbit,* etc.) as [brə] he must get this from independent knowledge of Negro dialect, not from any hint in Harris' pages. There is also

2. See Daniel Jones, An Outline of English Phonetics, 3d ed. Cambridge (1932). Many scholars find it more convenient to use phonetic script of their own devising.

3. See George P. Krapp, The English Language in America, 1. 225–273 (1925).

a certain amount of mere misspelling of standard English, as *sez* for *says*. About all we can grant the novelists is the basic observation that there are regional and class variations in speech.

50. During the past century or so there have been published a number of dictionaries and grammars of various local dialects.[4] Many of these works are excellent, both as collections of material and as descriptions of particular local dialects. In their very nature, however, they tend to be misleading. The dialects of any two towns at a distance of a hundred miles or more in a long-settled area will differ from each other in many respects; but if full information is secured about the distribution of all these features, it will usually be found that there is no sharp dialect boundary. Instead each feature of linguistic difference will tend to have its own boundary, which is technically known as an **isogloss**; [5] Figure 2 [6] is a map of the Rhine country, intersected by isoglosses between the Low German retention of voiceless stops, *k, p, t,* and the High German change of these to spirants or affricates (*ch, f* or *pf, s*). In this region there are five isoglosses, one dividing *ik* from *ich,* one *make* from *mache,* and others separating *Dorp* from *Dorf, dat* from *das,* and *Appel* from *Apfel.* Speakers in Essen say *ik, make, Dorp, dat,* and *Appel,* while natives of Strassburg say *ich, mache, Dorf, das,* and *Apfel.* Speakers in Düsseldorf say *ich,* but agree with their neighbors in Essen as to the other four words. The people of Cologne say *ich* and *mache* but *Dorp, dat,* and *Appel.* Natives of Koblenz say *Dorf* and those of Mainz say *das.* What is needed is a record of the geographic distribution of each linguistic feature; on the basis of such a record it may be possible to tie several isoglosses into a bundle, but as a rule dialect boundaries are not sharp.

51. Since 1876 techniques for collecting and recording local variations

4. We may mention J. A. Schmeller, Die Mundarten Bayerns, Munich (1821) [a partial reprint by O. Mausser (1929)]; Bayerisches Wörterbuch, 2d ed. Munich (1872–77); J. Wright, The English Dialect Dictionary, London (1898–1905); The English Dialect Grammar, Oxford (1905); Edwin Roedder, Volkssprache und Wortschatz des badischen Frankenlandes dargestellt auf Grund der Mundart von Oberschefflenz, New York (1936).

5. The weather maps registering maximum temperatures for a twenty-four-hour period are intersected by lines joining stations that reported the same maximum temperatures. These lines are called *isotherms.* The somewhat similar lines on dialect maps are named *isoglosses,* although they do not join places with the same linguistic feature, but separate places with contrasting features.

6. Simplified from Figure 20 in Adolf Bach, Deutsche Mundartforschung, p. 86, Heidelberg (1934). I am indebted to Bernard Bloch for the sketch.

of speech have been in process of development. In that year Georg Wenker began a survey of the German dialects around Düsseldorf. He later extended the area studied to include the entire German Empire. He had forty Standard German sentences translated into more than 40,000

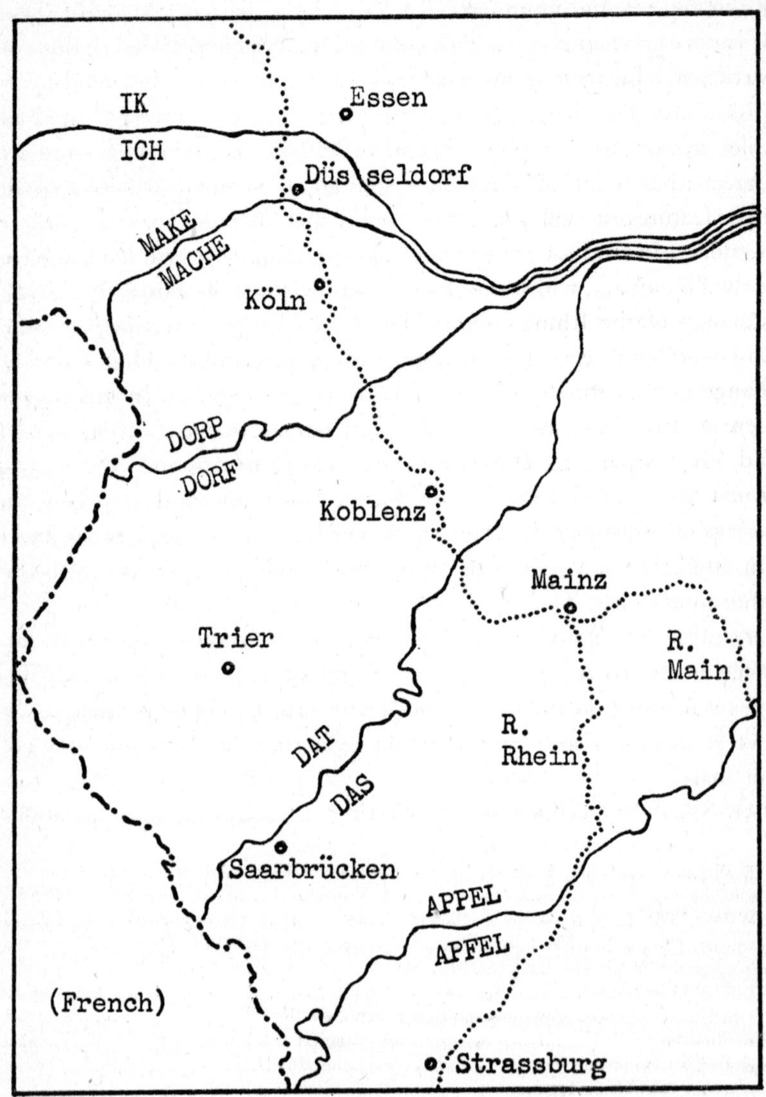

Figure 2.

local dialects. On the basis of this material it was possible to register on maps the distribution of a large number of linguistic features; the maps have been appearing in print since 1926.[7] The translating was done by a large number of men, few of whom had adequate linguistic training; the results are uneven in reliability, but the mass of the information provides the means of checking for errors. The science of linguistics promptly gained a new and important source.

52. The plan for the French atlas was radically different.[8] All the collecting was done by one man, Edmond Edmont, who was a trained phonetician, and who personally interviewed a native speaker in each village. This procedure necessarily limited the number of localities that could be investigated; instead of the 40,000 places recorded for the German atlas, the French atlas registers only a little more than 600. The informants were interviewed on the basis of a questionnaire of some 2,000 words and phrases. The results for phonetics and lexicon are more abundant than those secured by the German atlas, but the wide gaps between the points studied are unfortunate.

53. The Italian atlas[9] followed the plan of the French atlas in the main, but paid more attention to differences in culture that accompany differences in dialect. Another innovation was the practice of interviewing two informants from the cities, so as to record different cultural levels.

54. The plan for the New England atlas[10] was prepared with the assistance of the editors of the Italian atlas; and Jakob Jud and a field-worker, Paul Scheuermeier, assisted in training the original members of the New England staff. Instead of the single field-worker for the French atlas and the three who contributed to the Italian atlas, nine persons gathered material from New England. This made it possible to finish the field work within a period of twenty-five months.

Field reports were recorded in a phonetic alphabet based upon that of the International Phonetic Association with a number of additional signs and with a set of **shift-signs** for the vowels; if the vowel is articu-

7. F. Wrede, Deutscher Sprachatlas, Marburg (1926–).

8. J. Gilliéron and E. Edmont, Atlas linguistique de la France, Paris (1902–10), 35 parts.

9. Karl Jaberg and Jakob Jud, Sprach- und Sachatlas Italiens und der Südschweiz, Zofingen, Switzerland (1928–40), 16 vols.

10. Hans Kurath and Others, Linguistic Atlas of New England, Providence, R.I. (1939–43), 734 maps, 3 vols. in 6; Handbook of the Linguistic Geography of New England, Providence (1939).

lated a little higher than usual that fact is indicated by a following arrowhead pointed upward thus [oˆ] while a slightly fronted articulation is indicated by an arrowhead pointing to the left [o›]; similarly [oˇ] is a lowered [o], and [o›] is one articulated further back than usual. Great pains were taken to train all nine fieldworkers to use this delicate instrument as nearly as possible in the same way. Nevertheless the editors found characteristic differences for each one of them; an account of these differences is given in the Handbook in connection with the detailed account of the phonetic alphabet; within limits the reader can make allowances for the personal equation of the fieldworker.

A cardinal deviation from the practice of the French and Italian atlases was the use of two informants in the same locality, so as to record different age-groups. If this had been carried through consistently, it would have given virtually the same result as two atlases recorded, say, ten or fifteen years apart. As a matter of fact, however, the intervals in age are very uneven; in some cases the informant who represents the more conservative speech is actually younger than the less conservative speaker. The additional information obtained by this device is of very great value, but perhaps it would have been better to speed up the whole process in the hope of covering the ground again in the course of some twenty-five years. In all descriptive work, the best way to bring in the chronological factor is to compare two relatively complete and independent descriptions of the situation separated by a known interval of time.

The New England atlas follows the Italian atlas in recording an informant of relatively high education from certain important cities and towns.

55. The inclusion of two or three informants from a given locality and also the somewhat greater complication of the questionnaire emphasized a difficulty that had always been inherent in the plan of basing maps directly upon field reports. What is wanted is a set of maps each of which presents in striking form the geographic distribution of a single linguistic feature. If the feature studied is a matter of vocabulary sometimes nothing is needed but to print in the proper places the words reported from the informants. On the other hand, if there are several equivalent words in use and if two or three informants are recorded in each locality the resultant map may be quite confusing.

Phonetic and syntactic features, of course, never appear in pure form in the fieldworker's report; they have to be extracted from the words and sentences that have been taken down from the lips of the informant. And the publication of the material cannot wait for so complicated a process. What is printed is a series of maps upon which have been marked by number the several localities where informants live. On each map are printed, next the numbers, the answers to a single question, e.g., the pronunciation of the word *first*. An investigation of the treatment of postvocalic *r* must be based upon this map and also upon the maps recording the pronunciation of *work, girl, corn, father, rather,* etc.[11] Each of the maps is significant for other problems, *work* for the treatment of initial *w, father* for the vowel of the first syllable, etc. No one of the maps, as it stands, can be used for the pronunciation of a particular phoneme, both because it contains more than that and because its evidence has to be supplemented by other maps.

With rare exceptions, then, a linguistic atlas is a collection of raw material, from which a properly trained linguist can, by patient study, construct effective maps of the distribution of linguistic features. And for this task, a large map is a peculiarly difficult piece of apparatus to handle. It is far more convenient to have at hand a list of the items that are customarily printed on the maps, each preceded by a numeral designating a position on a key map. In other words, the most convenient format for primary publication of dialect materials is a collection of tables,[12] from which scholars can prepare maps. The remainder of the proposed Linguistic Atlas of the United States and Canada is to be just this.

LAPSES

56. Every person's speaking is disfigured by frequent "slips of the tongue." An usher at a wedding is said to have hurried up to a woman who had entered a pew reserved for the bridal party, and said, "Mardon me, padam; this pie is occupewed. May I sew you to a sheet?" The Rev. A. W. Spooner of Oxford became famous for such slips as *beary wenches* for *weary benches*. He is said to have begun a speech before a group

11. The results of such an investigation are outlined by Bernard Bloch, Acts of the Fourth International Congress of Linguists, pp. 195–199, Copenhagen (1938).

12. A volume on much this plan has actually been published; Gauchat, Jeanjaquet, and Tappolet, Tableaux phonétiques des patois suisses romands, relevés comparatifs d'environ 500 mots dans 62 patois-types, Neuchatel (1925).

of farmers: *I have never before addressed so many tons of soil.* Far more common are small displacements of a phoneme, as *apartmen int New York* for *apartment in New York, a will wind* for *an ill wind, Verínica* for *Verónica* (a girl's name). Blemishes like these are extremely common in the speech of all men; it may be doubted whether three consecutive sentences are often spoken without one of them. Some speakers rarely utter a single long sentence without several false starts and corrections.

We may define a lapse as an unintentional linguistic innovation.

Some lapses, such as Spoonerisms and childish *brunged* for *brought,* are almost always noticed by the hearers, either with amusement or with disapproval. Frequently the speaker himself detects his error and immediately corrects it; e.g., *somebody must have thrown a pitch . . . I mean a peach pit.* Less violent lapses, such as *frobably the first* for *probably* or *comfterble* for *comfortable* often pass unnoticed by speaker or hearer. Even the lapses that are noticed are customarily ignored in polite society. There are, to be sure, some persons whose attention is abnormally fixed upon the words rather than upon the topic under discussion, and they sometimes make a nuisance of themselves by pointing out the error and getting it laughed at or recorded before the business in hand is allowed to proceed. One should be kind to these people; they are either fools or linguists!

Any phenomenon as common as the lapse cannot safely be neglected by the relevant science, and we shall try later on to show in some detail that lapses are actually important for linguistic science. And just because they are unimportant for the practical use of language, the linguist must be at some pains to observe and collect them. Since, however, precise data are needed about the circumstances under which the lapse occurs, it is almost necessary for a man who makes extensive collections to interrupt all sorts of conversations while he finds out what the speaker intended to say and what other words and phrases occurred to him during the act of speech. When these items have been elicited by questioning and have been recorded, the thread of the conversation will have been broken—unless to be sure, a part of the company has carried it on while the linguist and his victim were engaged in making their record.

57. As far as I know only one man, Rudolf Meringer of the University

of Vienna, has published large collections of lapses.[13] I was not surprised to learn that Meringer was unpopular among his colleagues. Fortunately it is possible to use moderation in the quest; lapses are so common that a collector can afford to let many escape him—enough, at least, so that he need not lose friends. It is to be hoped that adequate collections for other languages than German will soon appear. At present I must rely largely on my own collections supplemented by observations of students and colleagues; I am particularly indebted to Bernard Bloch of Yale and Myles Dillon of the University of Chicago. Some valuable material was recorded in 1900 by H. H. Bawden, A Study of Lapses,[14] but it is combined with much that is irrelevant and some items of doubtful authenticity.

58. So far scholars have reported only lapses that can easily be detected by any alert observer; as far as our records go they consist entirely of phonemes current in the language concerned. In the nature of the case a lapse cannot be repeated; if the speaker who has just said *frobably the first* is asked to repeat he will say *probably,* or, if he has noticed his error, he will now say *frobably* with a normal *f* whether or not the original lapse contained this or an unusual sound between *p* and *f*. The observer therefore has just one chance to listen to a lapse, and that one chance always comes without warning. Of course the hearer, even if he be an expert phonetician, is sure, under such circumstances, to interpret what he hears as consisting of ordinary phonemes of the language.

59. It is probably possible to discover whether or not lapses include sub-phonemic assimilations. When *peach pit* (see above, § 56) yielded *pitch,* was the vowel something between English [i] and [ɪ]? If good mechanical records of lapses are played over repeatedly, it should be possible to answer such questions. No study of lapses on the basis of mechanical records has yet been undertaken. We know, however, that in the historical development of languages a phoneme frequently changes its phonetic character or even gives rise to two distinct phonemes; sub-phonemic lapses may perhaps be concerned in the process. Sub-phonemic assimilation is well attested in our literary and other texts (**§ 130. 2. 2**).

13. R. Meringer and K. Mayer, Versprechen und Verlesen, pp. 9–99, Stuttgart (1895); R. Meringer, Aus dem Leben der Sprache, pp. 11–120, Berlin (1908).

14. The Psychological Review, Monograph Supplements = Psychological Monographs 3, No. 4.

CHAPTER V

THE ORIGIN OF LANGUAGE

60. After much futile discussion linguists have reached the conclusion that the data with which they are concerned yield little or no evidence about the origin of human speech.[1] La Société de Linguistique de Paris has long had a standing rule that no papers on this subject may be presented at its sessions. The recorded history of language, even when supplemented by the prehistoric reconstructions of the comparative method (Chapter XV), covers only a small fraction of the development to which language has been subjected since its origin. We can learn from the total of our material a great deal about the later stages of this development, but it does not carry us appreciably nearer the beginning. Neither can we any longer expect the study of the speech of "primitive peoples" to shed light on the origin of speech; as far as we know there is no indication that any language spoken today has had a shorter history or a slower development than any other. Similarly the speech of young children has not so far yielded any clear results for our purpose. From birth children are under the influence of ordinary speech, which they proceed to imitate; if they ever strike out for themselves as the first speakers must have done, we can scarcely hope to identify these exploits.

61. There is, however, a vast amount of communication aside from language among animals as well as among men, and in spite of some fairly sharp distinctions there are similarities between language and all the rest of this material. It is not improbable that human gestures, dance, and song have developed out of the same complex of behavior that yielded language, and, although language has, throughout historic time, been our chief means of communication, the comparison of all four activities may be suggestive.

62. Much more hopeful is the comparison of the communicative behavior of other animals with that of man. This laborious task will neces-

1. See especially J. Vendryes, Language, a Linguistic Introduction to History, translated by Paul Radin, pp. 6 f., New York, (1925).

sarily fall mainly upon the zoologists, but they will have to learn from linguists and anthropologists what sort of things they should look for.

The following attempt to pick out some likenesses and differences between animal cries and human speech is elementary and obvious.[2] However, I hope that it will show that comparison of more abundant data is likely to be fruitful. I venture to follow it by a highly imaginative account of some possible first steps in the development of human speech out of something like the behavior of animals; I hope that none of my readers will take these details more seriously than I do.

63. First of all we may contrast the immense variability of human speech with the invariability and monotony of animal cries. No one knows how many languages there are in the world; there is not even perfect agreement about the number of languages to be assumed for such a well-known region as the Iberian Peninsula. There are groups of speakers who cannot understand each other, but contiguous local dialects differ so little that communication across every border is easy. Shall we then call Catalan, Castilian, and Portuguese three of the dialects of a single Iberian language? Or shall we be guided by literary considerations and call them three separate languages? Or shall we allow political geography to decide that while Portuguese is a separate language, Catalan and Castilian are two of the dialects of Spanish? It is extremely difficult to count languages even in case one has complete information, and for most parts of the world the available information is quite inadequate.

It is probably safe to say that the number of mutually unintelligible languages now spoken is above two thousand rather than below. Furthermore, in many parts of the world linguistic variety is known to have decreased since the beginning of historical records. In Italy of the third century B.C. there were at least three distinct languages belonging to the same group as Latin, namely, Faliscan of Falerii (thirty miles north of Rome), Oscan of Campania and Samnium, and Umbrian to the east of the upper Tiber, in addition to several dialects that were relatively close to Oscan or to Umbrian. Other Indo-European languages in the peninsula were Greek and Messapian in the south, Venetic near the northern end of the Adriatic, and Gaulish in the Valley of the Po. Etrus-

2. The general point of view was suggested by W. D. Whitney's chapter on the "Nature and Origin of Language" in his Life and Growth of Language, pp. 278–309, New York (1882).

can was spoken just across the Tiber from Rome, and Ligurian on the Gulf of Genoa. Besides we have brief inscriptions in several other languages. At present there are in Italy only dialects of Italian, except for a few villages in Calabria where the peasants speak Greek or Albanian. A similar situation has resulted wherever the Latin language was permanently established. The same thing is occurring on a large scale at present in many parts of the world; notably in Siberia, where Russian is being substituted for a host of languages of various groups, in Latin America, where the Indian languages slowly disappear before Spanish and Portuguese, and especially in the United States, where English is driving out the Indian languages and also many European and Asiatic languages temporarily established here. In North America, north of Mexico, the number of native languages has been reduced by something like 40 per cent since the coming of the Europeans.[3]

64. Every language of which we have adequate knowledge is divided into several dialects; when the Natchez language of Oklahoma was first recorded a few years ago, it was spoken by one old man and one old woman, who used different dialects. If we try to take account of all significant local variations in such a language as English, it is quite impossible to count them; at the very least there are many hundreds. And if we could recover the speech of Shakespeare's time, it is certain that no one of the English dialects of the present day could be found in its present form. Human speech is infinitely variable both in time and in space.

Furthermore, each man's use of his language is extremely varied. Gifted authors produce many books whose contents differ enough to attract many readers, and no man sets down on paper more than a small fraction of what he says. In fact, it is rarely possible to predict accurately what a man will say in any given situation. Bloomfield[4] illustrates the use of human speech as follows:

> Suppose Jack and Jill are walking down a lane. Jill is hungry. She sees an apple in a tree. She makes a noise with her larynx, tongue, and lips. Jack vaults the fence, climbs the tree, takes the apple, brings it to Jill, and places it in her hand. Jill eats the apple.

3. Voegelin, Indian Languages Still Spoken = Language, Culture, and Personality (1941), p. 29, says: ". . . it seems safe to estimate that well over half the aboriginal languages are still spoken."

4. Language, p. 22.

Even assuming that Jack and Jill spoke some form of standard English, it would have been impossible to predict what words Jill would have used.

65. Animal cries on the contrary are strikingly uniform, both within a given species and in the performance of any individual. A given species is always recognizable by its characteristic voice if it utters any sound at all; it doesn't matter where or under what circumstances the animal is born and grows up. There is nothing about animal cries analogous to the local and national differences in languages. Although we have no satisfactory records of animal cries in past ages, there are several well-known passages in ancient literature that have a meaning only if we assume that certain animals made noises closely similar to those we hear today. When a woman in Plautus, Menaechmi, 650–654, upbraids her husband with a repeated *tū, tū* 'you, you,' he offers to get her an owl, *quae "tū, tū" usque dicat tibi* "to keep saying *'tū, tū'* for you." Lucilius, 9. 377 f. M., says: "This cacophonous *r* isn't much different from saying in dogs' language, 'It's nothing to me.'" The ancient Greek comic poets indicated a sheep's cry by the letters *βη* whose value was approximately [bæ·]. This syllable has regularly changed to [vi] in Modern Greek, and so we may conclude at least that the Greek language has changed more than a sheep's cry in some two thousand years.

66. From the world-wide invariability of the cries of animals we must conclude that they are not learned solely by imitation. Imitation necessarily varies in accuracy, and any activity transmitted from generation to generation by this means alone is sure to change. It is familiar experience that a kitten or a puppy reared by hand, quite apart from others of his kind, develops the same cries as the rest of the species. Experiments on and observations of animal behavior show that animals do not readily imitate one another; monkeys and apes are more like man in this respect—they learn much by imitation—but it is not known that they imitate sounds at all.[5]

It follows that animal cries cannot have the arbitrary meanings that characterize human speech. Arbitrary meanings are necessarily a social matter, and can be transmitted only by imitation. The imitating birds,

5. E. L. Thorndike, Animal Intelligence, New York (1911); Robert M. Yerkes and Blanche M. Learned, Chimpanzee Intelligence and Its Vocal Expressions, Baltimore (1925); W. N. and L. A. Kellogg, The Ape and the Child, New York (1933), indexes s.v. *imitation.*

to be sure, differ from other animals in producing sounds by imitation, but they do not acquire any such wealth of speech forms as the least gifted of human speakers employ, and they attach no arbitrary meanings to their words. Anyone who expects to carry on a conversation with a parrot is going to be disappointed.

67. Equally remarkable is the monotony of an animal's vocal response to a given situation. We cannot predict what words Jill will use to induce Jack to bring her the apple. Still less can we tell what a poet will say in the presence of a beautiful sunrise or when he is disappointed in love. But we know pretty well what the cock will say at dawn or the hen when she has laid an egg. What will the pigs say when men are seen near the trough at feeding time? How will a cow call her calf? What will a dog say at the approach of his master? Or at the approach of a stranger? Of course no man can predict infallibly in such cases; the animal may say nothing at all, and there are considerable variations in loudness, in the persistence of the cry, and in other details. The remarkable thing, in view of our inability to predict human speech, is that we can predict animal cries at all.

It follows that the animals express only the grosser features of the situation. The cock does not tell us anything about the colors in the sky at dawn, or suggest that it will be a fine day. Neither does he imply that it is or is not time to get up. Just what feature of the situation he is reacting to we cannot discover, except that it must be some feature that is common to most dawns.

68. Each animal cry is comparatively simple. A bird's tune is soon finished, although it may be repeated immediately. Only rarely is there a change in character during the continuance of a single cry, except for the regular change required by the tune or other pattern, and when such a change occurs it reflects some change in the situation. If a dog is whining by the door and footsteps are heard on the other side of the door, the whine ceases and a bark may be substituted.

We are forced to conclude that there can be no such analytic structure as characterizes most speech. A single long blast of a whistle furnishes no basis for analysis, whereas a series of longer and shorter blasts may represent the Morse alphabet.

In this respect the unanalyzable parts of speech, such as most interjections, resemble animal cries. Furthermore, when analytic phrases come to be used as interjections, they frequently lose their analytic structure; English *goodby!* is all that is left from *god be with you.*

69. As to the meaning of animal cries, we cannot get beyond inferences. Nevertheless some such inferences are made by all men who have much to do with animals; and it is found that actions based upon these inferences are, as a rule, pragmatically justified. If I hear a hen cackle in a certain way, and then search for a new laid egg, I shall probably find one.

The exclamatory parts of language, like many animal cries, are characterized by extreme variations of pitch and loudness. This fact, added to the simplicity of the situations that induce them, makes them easy to understand. It is said that a group of Americans once hired some Neapolitan boatmen to row them out to a ship anchored in the bay. Midway in the journey the boatmen stopped rowing and demanded more money. One of the Americans, who spoke Italian, reminded them that a bargain had been made and accepted by both parties, and that the Americans had already performed their part. His words had no effect. Then another member of the party, who didn't know Italian, but who had been foreman of a construction gang on an American railroad, stood up and said in English what he thought of them. The men bent to their oars and finished the journey.

Whether this story is true or not, there is abundant experience to show that the expression of emotion by gesture, facial expression, and voice, or by any one of them alone, is immediately intelligible. In the same way men who have much to do with animals have little or no difficulty in recognizing mating calls and other courtship behavior. Similarly well known are cries of fear, of rage, and of victory. There is abundant proof that other animals of the same species respond to these calls roughly as men respond to the highly emotional features of languages.

If we go on to say that animal cries express emotion, that is, of course, an inference from the experience of men; but in the absence of conflicting evidence it seems to be highly plausible. At any rate men and animals make noises during love-making, fighting, flight, and victory; in men these activities involve emotion. Among men, furthermore, such noises are often as incapable of analysis as any animal cry, but, on the other hand, articulate speech may accomplish much the same thing.

When Jill saw the apple, perhaps she merely said, "Yum, yum!" But she may have said, "What a lovely apple!" or "I bet that apple would taste good!"

70. Again, pigs raise a din at feeding time. A shepherd dog yips at the heels of the flock. A hen clucks to her chicks at sight of a hawk, and the chicks run to cover beneath her wings, or, at a louder cry, they scatter among the bushes. Such cries obviously do much the same work as our imperatives; if I impute desire to them that is another inference from human experience. Jill may have expressed her desire for the apple by an imperative: "Jack, get me that apple."

71. Recognition is often a necessary prerequisite to an animal cry, just as recognition of the stall or of the water trough or of the prey is a necessary prerequisite to other kinds of animal behavior. In a sense, then, we may say that recognition may be expressed by an animal cry; I may conclude from a watchdog's bark or a rattlesnake's warning that I have been seen. A dog greets his master with one kind of a bark, a stranger with a very different kind. Mating calls involve, among other things, recognition of an animal of identical species and opposite sex; every farm boy knows the characteristic cry of the bull when he sees a cow, perhaps a quarter of a mile away.

Our emotional speech often involves the same sort of recognition. We do not say [ts, ts] (with suction) unless we recognize some specific occurrence. Before we say [š] we recognize a noise. These interjections resemble animal cries in their non-analytic structure and in their combination of recognition with emotion. Animal cries are not known ever to carry the relatively unemotional recognition contained in such sentences as *It's a horse, That's young wheat,* or *There it is again.*

72. There is no other part of the meaning of human speech that seems to be conveyed by animal cries. Emotion, then, is apparently expressed by animals, although certainly not in such fine nuances as language is capable of. Desires, including hunger and thirst, are among the emotions that we can infer from the noises made by animals, and fear is another. These emotions occur in situations in which men would use imperatives, and so we may perhaps say that animal cries may be commands or requests. Since many emotional cries are clearly conditioned by recognition of a previously experienced feature of the situation, we may, in a sense, say that animal cries express recognition. All the rest seems to belong to human speech alone.

73. If, then, we take animal cries as our starting point and assume that language developed out of something similar to them, we are confronted with these and similar problems. How did the ordered variety of our phonemic systems grow out of the disorderly monotony of animal cries? How did the meanings of most speech-forms come to be arbitrary? How did linguistic structure develop out of the undifferentiated or slightly differentiated cry? I am confident that none of these things could happen until the peculiarly human situation had been established that lies at the basis of Bloomfield's story of Jack and Jill. The essence of the story is that, instead of trying to reach the apple, Jill spoke to Jack and he got the apple; speech took the place of a handling reaction. When pigs squeal about the trough they are not asking anyone to get their food for them; they are doing their best to get it for themselves. Says Whitney: [6]

> Nor is it less plain what inaugurates the conversion <of natural expression into language>, and becomes the main determining element in the whole history of production of speech; it is the desire of communication. This turns the instinctive into the intentional. As itself becomes more distinct and conscious, it lifts expression of all kinds above its natural basis, and makes of it an instrumentality; capable, as such, of indefinite extension and improvement. He who (as many do) leaves this force out of account, cannot but make shipwreck of his whole linguistic philosophy. Where the impulse to communication is wanting, no speech comes into being.

74. The gap between the meaningful behavior of animals and human speech is indeed very wide; at present, available evidence does not furnish a bridge. It is not difficult, however, to invent more or less plausible incidents that might have facilitated the crossing.[7]

A woman once found a bush laden with ripe fruit, satisfied her hunger, and went in search of her child. When she found him she was still showing signs of satiety—stroking her abdomen, perhaps. These signs,

6. Life and Growth, pp. 283 f.

7. What follows is a revision of part of an article published in the Classical Weekly, 16. 34–38 (1922).

correctly interpreted by the child, led him to look about for the food. Hitherto the mother had led the way to the berries and had plucked them for the child, but today she was languid after a full meal, and the bush was near by. So she made as if to reach for the berries, whereupon the child ran off in the indicated direction. For the first time the woman had pointed for the sake of communication.

A man had frequently when angry beaten his mate or shaken his fist at her, had read the signs of fear on her face, and had seen her submit to his will. One day it suited his purpose to cross a swollen stream, and his mate was afraid to venture into it. He realized the danger, and doubted whether she could reach the other bank; he was not angry at all. Nevertheless he shook his fist at her in order to drive her into the water; he used a gesture to convince her that he was angry.

One detail of these two imaginary communications must be correct; both were insincere. The mother pretended that she was going to pluck berries when she had no intention of doing so, and the man feigned anger which he did not feel. All real intentions and emotions got themselves expressed involuntarily, and as yet nothing but intention and emotion had called for expression. So voluntary communication can scarcely have been called upon except to deceive; language must have been invented for the purpose of lying.[8] When once the intent to com-

8. My brother, Alfred H. Sturtevant, has convinced me that the insincere expression of emotion must be ascribed to other animals than man. He refers to Wallace Craig, Journal of Comparative Neurology and Psychology, 19. 33 (1909): "The blue jay . . . often gives alarming cries when no danger is near, and seems to enjoy . . . the consternation which it can thus produce among its feathered neighbors."

My brother adds: "Cocks make a special noise when they find food, and other fowls come running and help eat it. I have often observed them make this noise—plus the associated pecking movements—when no food was present; one of my colleagues confirms this observation. But I have also observed that, when the false call is given, the cock will sometimes attempt to mate with a hen that has been attracted.

"A highly critical friend and colleague of mine reports that he once owned two dogs, each of which had a mat to sleep on. The older dog usually went to sleep first; but the younger preferred the mat belonging to the older. When he went to lie down he would approach the older one, then go and lie on his own mat. After a few moments he would bristle, growl, and start up. Both dogs would then start, rushing and barking, to the door; but the younger would immediately break off, and run straight to the mat vacated by the older, and lie on it. My friend reports this as a frequently repeated affair.

"I suppose both of these cases can reasonably be interpreted as rather complex conditioned reflexes, accidental in their origin; but they do seem to me to indicate that the business of using sounds for 'purposeful' lying may occur below the human level."

I have nevertheless left the text unchanged. Apparently this sort of cheating has had no further development among animals other than man.

municate had become familiar, men no doubt renewed or intensified the expression of genuine emotion when other men approached. Just so children cry louder if they have an audience. Thus after a while lying lost its exclusive vogue.

75. Side by side with the expression of emotion, which was becoming more and more largely voluntary, the imitation of sights and sounds was constantly cultivated. It must have been among man's chief amusements, as it is to this day in the highly developed forms which we know as art, music, and drama. Human skill of this sort was early turned to account in decoying birds by the imitation of their cries, or in driving off wolves or elephants by the imitation of the lion's roar.

Once a hunter met a lion in the forest, climbed the nearest tree, and escaped with an ugly gash in his leg. Some time later he was found by a friend, and he made known his plight by renewed groans. The friend looked about for the cause of the accident, whereupon the wounded hunter satisfied the newcomer's curiosity by repeating the lion's roar. Again a step forward in the development of language! He had communicated information as distinct from emotion. And there was a vast store of imitative material at hand for doing just this.

76. 1. Perhaps the next important improvement was the combination of simple elements into a complex communication. A hunter who had found aboundant game gave the hunting call. The others hesitated whether to arm themselves with small stones, large stones, or clubs, and so the bringer of the news imitated the cry of quail. Thereafter the hunting call was often coupled with an indication of the character of the game; hunting call plus quail's cry meant approximately 'hunt quail.'

76. 2. Then must have followed the analogical analysis of the more elaborate of the imitations that had long been current. A man who howled like a wolf and galloped on all fours was understood to say 'wolf runs'; just as the imitation of the note was the name of the quail in the model sentence, so the wolf's howl was taken to be the name of the wolf in the sentence now analyzed.[9] With this much accomplished, the development of an elaborate syntax would be only a matter of time.

9. Of course the distribution of the elements may as well have been the reverse. The maker of the first sentence may have named an animal by imitating his gait instead of his cry, and so the newly analyzed sentence would mean 'wolf howls.'

76.3. As intentional communication became more and more common, a process of abbreviation and conventionalization must have set in. In order to tell of the pains suffered some days ago the groans need not last as long as they had then; one groan would be enough. Neither was it necessary to repeat the intonation or the loudness of the original groans; perhaps a mere *ouch* would do. Perhaps *mi-au-u,* the original word for 'cat,' was shortened to *mew* or the like. Just so significant gestures were shortened and conventionalized until they had no recognizable appropriateness; and so in time words and gestures came to have only traditional or arbitrary connection with their meaning.

76.4. In the meantime symbols of all sorts took on new meanings. Certain women, perhaps, were called *mew,* and certain men were characterized by drawing a wavy line on the ground—the proper symbol for 'snake.' The extended open palm meant 'give,' and so the drawn back closed fist came to mean 'keep' in addition to its earlier meaning 'threaten.' So vocabulary was gradually built up.

77. Before this process had gone far another fundamental improvement must have set in. Originally there were many synonyms; the 'elephant' might be denoted by his cry, by imitating his swaying gait, by some gesture imitating the animal's trunk, or by a combination of these. The easiest of all the symbols to make was the cry; and the cry alone could be used in the dark, or when the recipient of the communication had his back turned. Finally the cry alone left the arms and legs free for another occupation. So sounds were again and again preferred to gestures, and presently sounds were substituted for gestures where these had at first been the only symbols in use.

This we may characterize as the last step essential to the origin of language. Once communication had become chiefly vocal, and meanings might be quite arbitrary, and a beginning had been made at syntactic structure, language such as we know could develop by processes actually observed in linguistic history.

CHAPTER VI

DESCRIPTIVE LINGUISTICS

78. **Descriptive linguistics** forms the basis for **historical linguistics;** you cannot treat the history of a language until you know several stages of that language. Comparative linguistics likewise should be based upon a description of several different languages. In short, grammatical science should logically proceed from descriptive, through historical, to comparative grammar.

The history of linguistics in Europe and America has oddly enough been just the reverse. Scientific treatment of language in Europe arose when men who were steeped in the grammatical technique of the Greeks and Romans learned the linguistic science of the Hindus. Both of these systems were, in the main, descriptive; the Hindu grammarians started with the minute description of the language of the Vedic hymns and went on to a description of the later form of the language, known as Sanskrit. The Greek grammarians similarly started with Homer and proceeded to the literary dialects of classical times. Although, in both countries, different stages of the language were considered, the treatment was descriptive rather than historical.

79. And yet the new discipline that arose from the contact of Greek grammar with Hindu grammar was **comparative** grammar. This was because everyone supposed that the descriptive work both in Europe and in India had already been done; the new and startling fact that galvanized the attention of scholars was the obvious relationship of Sanskrit with Greek and Latin. To quote once more the famous remark of Sir William Jones, Sanskrit bears to Greek and Latin "a stronger affinity, both in the roots of verbs and in the forms of grammar, than could possibly have been produced by accident; so strong, indeed, that no philologer could examine all three without believing them to have sprung from some common source."[1] And so scholars proceeded to work out the details of the "affinity" between Sanskrit and the earliest known forms of the European languages.

1 Asiatick Researches, 1. 422 f. (1788).

80. Only by slow degrees did scientific curiosity awaken in regard to later stages of European languages and to other "cultivated" languages of the Old World. Still more recently have scholars followed missionaries and explorers in studying the languages of primitive peoples. Now all are agreed that every type of human speech deserves scientific description regardless of the length of its known history, and a start has been made in providing reliable grammars and dictionaries for the thousands of languages now spoken on earth. The overwhelming majority, however, have never been described at all or only by amateurs and in a way that provides no safe foundation for linguistic science.

81. The description of a language falls into three parts: grammar (including phonetics and phonemics), lexicography, and stylistic. Each of these consists essentially of an account of forms or groups of forms and of the meanings that are carried by them. The lines of division are not sharp; in actual practice lexicography treats of the words of a language as separate entities, and grammar covers the rest of the material, except style; but it is impossible to treat any part of morphology or syntax without discussing words, and a word cannot be fully described without an account of its function in the sentence. We can more accurately describe a grammar as a set of general statements (paradigms and rules) and lists of exceptions; while a lexicon contains the material that cannot conveniently be combined into general statements.[2] Stylistic treats of the selection among the linguistic responses possible in a given situation. It shows how one man will use certain words and syntactic constructions where another man will employ a more or less different linguistic mechanism. It also shows that different situations call for different words and phrases quite aside from the obvious requirements of meaning.

2. Bloomfield, Language, p. 161, describes a **morpheme** as one of the forms that remain when grammatical analysis has been completed (in this book we say, as the case may be, *root* or *stem, prefix, infix, suffix*). On the following page he says: "The total stock of morphemes in a language is its *lexicon.*" Such a lexicon would presumably be supplemented by a grammar which would treat the structure and the combination of the morphemes. A Latin lexicon of this sort would not include the word *urbānus,* but would contain the morphemes *urb-, āno-,* and *-s;* for an account of such words as *urbs, urbānus,* and *suburbānus* one would apparently have to refer to the grammar. Of course Bloomfield knows that such a lexicon as that has not been published for any language. Perhaps the nearest approach to it is provided by the inclusion of prefixes, suffixes, and inflectional endings in certain English dictionaries, but even these list many words that can be analyzed.

SCHOOL GRAMMARS

82. Most of our school grammars must be classed as descriptive. They are intended as helps in learning a language, and each language, at any moment in its history, is a definite system of forms employed in a definite way; for its users a language is static, although it is actually changing all the time. Traditional grammars, however, usually fall short of being consistently descriptive in one or more of these five ways.

82.1. Many school grammars treat of several stages of a language at once. Latin grammars are chiefly devoted to Ciceronian and Augustan Latin, and this furnishes a reasonably unitary basis; but they also treat of the Early Latin of Plautus and Terence and of the Imperial Latin of Seneca, Tacitus, and their successors. The triple task might be handled descriptively by means of separate paragraphs; but most authors trace the development of one usage into another, thereby blurring the picture. Some Latin grammars even include irrelevant remarks about comparative grammar.

82.2. Most school grammars of Greek are based upon the Attic dialect, but nearly all of them have something to say about other dialects. Again it is customary to include some of the history implied by dialectic differences. It is possible to describe several dialects together without confusing the reader, but the task requires great skill.

82.3. The analysis of any language brings to light a great deal of logic. Here is an example. The Latin accusative is primarily based upon form. The category consists of certain nominal and pronominal forms including noun forms which are marked by certain endings; the precise formal description is necessarily complicated, and the school grammars distribute it over many pages, but they finally include all of it well enough. The uses of the Latin accusative are extremely varied, but more than half of them may be assigned to one logical category—that to which a motion is directed or upon which an action impinges, the **goal.** A very little study of Latin texts reveals logical subdivisions of this category. *Rōmam amat* 'he loves Rome' and *Rōmam venit* 'he comes to Rome' involve different relationships between verb and noun; our grammars call the first *Rōmam* a direct object and the second an accusative of the end of motion; and this distinction actually belongs to Latin grammar, because in the nearly equivalent sentences *urbem* *amat* and *ad urbem venit* the distinction has formal expression. As it is put in our grammars, the accusative of the end of motion without a preposition is confined to names of towns and certain other words. There is an equally clear logical distinction between the sentences *domum amat* 'he is fond of the house' and *domum aedificat* 'he builds the house,' since in the second sentence the house owes its very existence to the activity stated by the verb. This latter type of accusative has by some been erected into a separate grammatical category—accusative of the inner object; but the distinction is not a part of Latin grammar, since it has no formal expression in this or any similar Latin sentence.[3]

All men learn much of the logic they customarily use from the structure of their native language, but we have no right to ascribe to any language a logical distinction which it leaves unexpressed.

82. 4. Since English has usually been described in the terminology of Latin grammar, English has often been said to have a dative case with several different forms, those, namely, that may translate a Latin dative, (a) the first of two objects (*he gave him the book*), (b) a phrase with *to* (*he gave the book to him*), and (c) a phrase with *for* (*he brought the book for him*). Another way of forcing English into the Latin mold is to rule out English expressions which do not follow a Latin model. Such a sentence as *the boy is given the book* is quite common in present-day English,[4] but it has often been condemned by grammarians who would tie the English down to the Latin alternatives: *librum puero dat* or *liber puero datur.* Many generations of school teachers have struggled against *it's me; me, I like coffee,* and the like, with only one sign of success: they have induced the children to say *he saw you and I.*

The grammatical description of each language must be based upon that language. The numerous attempts to write a universal grammar into which the forms of each language could be fitted are quite fantastic; languages differ in their structure no less than in their words.

82. 5. Perhaps the most serious fault of many school grammars is the attempt to brand certain speech forms as incorrect. Since all language is arbitrary, whatever speech is current in the community is necessarily

3. Of course the logical distinction can be stated in Latin, much as we have stated it in English; but its expression is never required by Latin grammar.

4. Examples in Jespersen, A Modern English Grammar, 3. 305, Heidelberg (1927).

correct; aside from lapses (§ 56) only a foreigner can speak incorrectly. When English teachers condemn *it's me,* they are trying to foist Latin grammar upon the language; and when they condemn *ain't,* they are promoting a certain class dialect.

VARIATION IN LINGUISTIC STRUCTURE

83. The most familiar classification of languages is into three groups, known as **isolating, agglutinating,** and **inflecting** respectively. The type specimen of isolating languages is Chinese, whose words are strung together in a sentence without change of form. The Chinese sentence *wǒ pú p'à t'ā* [5] may be closely imitated in English, if we use the form *me* for 'I' as well as for 'me,' thus: *me not fear him.* Just so, if we use *him* for 'he' as well as for 'him,' we may translate Chinese *t'ā pú p'à wǒ* as *him not fear me.* Both these Chinese sentences and both these made-up English sentences exhibit isolating structure. The difference between the two languages is that what we can occasionally do in English is typical of Chinese. It is customary to add that all Chinese words are monosyllabic and that the language is quite without word derivation, but both these statements are false. For example, although *tūng-hsi* 'thing' consists of two syllables, each of which may function as a word, that is purely accidental; *tūng* means 'east' and *hsī* 'west'! The composition of two adjectives denoting opposed qualities, such as 'high' and 'low,' yields a quality noun, meaning 'height' or the like. There is a suffix *-ch'u* '-ness' that is freely attached to adjectives, e.g., *hǎu* 'good,' *hǎuch'u* 'goodness,' *ch'áng* 'long,' *ch'ángch'u* 'length.' It is true, however, that Chinese has a large proportion of monosyllabic words and relatively little in the way of composition and derivation.

84. The agglutinating languages are those like Turkish or Finnish that have relatively long words built up in much the fashion of the Chinese sentence. In Turkish there is an elaborate declension, which may be illustrated by these forms:

ev 'house'
ev-den 'from a house'
ev-im 'my house'

5. The accent marks indicate the tones: ¯ = level tone, ´ = rising tone, ˇ = dipping tone, ` = falling tone. For these remarks on Chinese, I am indebted to George Kennedy.

ev-im-den 'from my house'
ev-ler 'houses'
ev-ler-den 'from houses'
ev-ler-im 'my houses'
ev-ler-im-den 'from my houses'

These agglutinative elements are subject to certain regular changes according to the phonetic character of the preceding syllable; from *oda* 'room' we get *oda-m-dan* 'from my room,' and *oda-lar-dan* 'from rooms.' The Turkish verb is similarly composed of agglutinative elements; *de* means 'say' (imperative), *de-yor* 'he is saying,' *de-yor-lar* 'they are saying,' *de-yecek̦* 'he will say,' *de-yecek̦-ler* 'they will say.'

The fundamental difference between Chinese structure and Turkish structure is that in the former language the tacking together of relatively short invariable elements extends from beginning to end of every sentence, while the Turkish sentence is normally composed of several words of varying length, some of which consist of short elements.

85. Inflecting languages are typified by the older Indo-European and Semitic languages, and inflecting structure is still common in the modern Indo-European languages, including English. Not a little of this material is very similar in structure to what we have already observed in the Chinese sentence and in certain Turkish words. Latin *amābāmus* is analyzed as *amā-* 'love,' *-bā-* (sign of the imperfect indicative), and *-mus* 'we.' Similarly Sanskrit *sunóti* 'he presses out' consists of the root *su-*, the present sign *-no-*, and the ending of the third person singular *-ti*. The corresponding plural form is to be analyzed *su-nv-ánti*, with a regularly alternating form *-nu-* (before a vowel *-nv-*) for the present suffix. The Indo-European and Semitic languages display much more variation in the grammatical elements than Turkish does; Sanskrit has many present suffixes, and it has almost as much variety in forming aorists. Besides, internal variation in the root often plays an important part in inflection, as in English *sing, sang, sung* or in Akkadian *ak̦áš̌ad* 'I reach,' *ák̦šud* 'I reached,' *k̦ášidu* 'reaching.'

86. Many sentences in Modern English approach the isolating structure of Chinese, and some can be completely analyzed in the Chinese fashion; e.g., *the man will fear the dog,* or (except for the *-s* of the verb forms) *the man pumps well water, the water spouts from the pump, the pump in the well spouts water, the pump waters the field.*

87. French phrases of a very familiar type are easily analyzed in the fashion of Turkish words; *je donne, je le donne, je le lui donne, je ne lui en donne pas, il donne, il me donne, il m'en donne, il ne m'en donne pas.* While many of these monosyllabic or less than syllabic elements may freely be alternated or omitted, they can stand in no other order, and no insertions or substitutions are possible outside of the small group of monosyllables that belong to the system. The only important difference from Turkish is in the verb, which stands at or near the end of the cluster; *donne* alternates with *donnons, a donné,* etc., and any one of a considerable list of verbs may be used instead of this one.

88. No sentence in any language tells all that can be told about a situation. For instance, the sentence *the man pumps well water* does not tell whether the man is young or old, tall or short; it leaves us uninformed about the color of his skin and hair and the character of his clothing. We do not know whether the weather is hot or cold, in what part of the world the work is being done, or even whether the speaker is a witness of it. Neither do we know what kind of a pump is used or how deep the well is or what sort of water it produces. We do not even know whether the pumping is going on at this moment; perhaps it is an habitual operation by a man who just now is asleep. Any of these things can be told in any language, but no language is likely to tell many of them about any one occurrence.

English requires us to tell whether the pumping is done by one man or several, unless we choose another kind of phrase (*one or more men pump; water is pumped*). Chinese, on the contrary, normally employs the word for 'man' without any indication of number, although it is quite possible to say 'one man' or 'two men' or 'several men.' Some languages provide a dual number, or even a dual and a trial, in addition to a plural.

Many other scraps of information about objects or persons mentioned are required by one language or another. Some languages must ordinarily indicate the general shape of objects (round, oblong, square, etc.); others must tell whether an object or a person is visible to the speaker or not.

89. Certain languages classify things as animate or inanimate, certain others as personal or impersonal. The Semitic languages, like modern French, make all nouns either masculine or feminine. The early Indo-

European languages had a triple classification (masculine, feminine, neuter), and this survives in some languages, such as German, to this day. Elsewhere, as in Modern Persian, the gender classification has been totally lost. In English we have a few traces of it in the pronouns and an occasional personification (*she* of a ship). In the Bantu languages of South Africa [6] there are several formally distinguished classes of nouns—in some dialects as many as twenty. Some of the classes carry plural meaning, but in large part the assignment of a noun to one class or another seems quite arbitrary. A similar statement can be made of French, German, or Latin gender classes, and of the Algonquian animate class, which includes words for *kettle, knee, maize, bean,* and *tobacco.* Typically arbitrary is the German assignment of the words for 'knife,' 'fork,' and 'spoon' to three different genders and the neuter gender of many diminutives from personal nouns. A very common feature of such noun classes is agreement (concord) with them on the part of other words in the sentence. In the Bantu languages a reminder of the noun-class of the subject is prefixed to every important word in the sentence, and, with certain exceptions, the Semitic verb, as well as the adjective, agrees with the subject in gender.

90. English requires us to use some tense, and the present tense usually means that the action is occurring now or will occur in the future or that it occurs repeatedly. Chinese, on the other hand, normally uses a verb without any specific suggestion of time, unless a speaker adds a word for 'now' or 'yesterday' or the like. Some languages require even more subdivisions of time than English does; Wishram, an Indian language of the Pacific Northwest, distinguishes between recent past, remote past, and mythological past.

91. Russian verb forms all belong to one of the three formally distinguished **aspects: durative, momentaneous,** or **iterative;** English *pity* is translated by a durative, *take pity on* by a momentaneous form, and English *beat* by an iterative. The peculiarity of Russian is that every verb must belong to one or another of the three categories; there are no verbs like English *love, strike, ride,* which do not compel the speaker to decide this particular question. We do, to be sure, have an English phrase by which the Russian durative can frequently be translated,

6. See Jespersen, Language, pp. 352–355, New York (1922), and references.

namely, the verb *be* with the present participle, but the correspondence is only partial, and aside from that the English language does not require any distinction similar to the Russian aspects.

More or less similar are some distinctions made by the ancient Greek verb, which has a durative past, commonly called the imperfect, (*apethnēiske* 'he was dying'), a non-durative past, known as the aorist, (*apethane* 'he died'), and a present resultative, called the perfect, (*tethnēke* 'he is dead').

Latin has a durative past, the imperfect, and a non-durative past, the perfect. From a few verbs an iterative can be formed, e.g., *cantō* 'I (often) sing' from *canō, rogitō* 'I keep asking' from *rogō, dictitō* 'I assert repeatedly' from *dictō* 'assert.' The last named verb is similarly formed from *dīcō* 'say,' but it does not have the iterative meaning. The few iterative verbs of Latin are not comparable to the Russian iteratives; their description, like that of English *beat,* belongs rather to the lexicon than to the grammar.

92. Languages differ also in the fundamental classification of their words; many languages lack some or most of the parts of speech that must be assumed for English and Latin. In Kota, a Dravidian language spoken in the hills of southern India, there is no class of adjectives separate from the nouns. Instead, a noun preceding another noun may designate a characteristic of the second, as if one should say in English *strength-man* for *strong man.*

Probably a majority of languages have classes of words more or less like our nouns or verbs, but many languages have no such categories. Nootka, a language of Vancouver Island,[7] has inflectional forms that may conveniently be called nominal or verbal, but neither its roots nor any entire groups of its inflectional forms can be classified as nouns or verbs. The radical element *inikw-* means 'fire' or 'burn' according to the context. Just so *inikw-ihl* means either 'fire in the house' or 'burn in the house.' This may receive a plural suffix *-ʔminih,* a diminutive suffix *-ʔis,* and a preterit suffix *-it,* and it remains neither noun nor verb; but at any point one may append either the suffixed article *-ʔi* and procure a noun, or an indicative suffix and get a verb; *inikw-ʔi* means 'the fire,'

7. This passage is abbreviated from Sapir, Language, pp. 109 f. and 141 f., New York (1921).

inikw-ma 'it burns'; *inikw-ihl-ʔminih-ʔis-it-ʔi* means 'the former small fires in the house,' and *inikwihlʔminihʔisit-a* 'several small fires were burning in the house.'

In Tagalog, the Philippine language of Manila,[8] the same forms may in general serve as subject or as predicate. The two functions are determined in part by position in the sentence but chiefly by certain prefixed particles. Thus a prefixed *ang* [ɑŋ] determines a nominal use, and either initial position or a prefixed *ay* marks a predicative use. E.g., *sumùsúlat ang bátaʔ* or *ang bátaʔ ay sumùsúlat* 'the child is writing.' We are prevented from calling *sumùsúlat* a verb by the fact that with prefixed *ang* it functions as a noun; *ang sumùsúlat ay si Pedro,* 'the person writing is Pedro.'

FUNCTIONAL MEANING[9]

93. In attempting to define a language (§ 3) we called it a system of symbols, and we noticed that a symbol is necessarily a dualism; in the case of a language the symbols consist of form and meaning. Linguistic science necessarily starts from the study of form. The meanings of all the utterances of a linguistic community cover the total experience of that community; they include the subject-matter of all the arts and sciences as well as all the practical occupations, amusements, and personal and family life. One science cannot successfully treat so much. Two divisions of linguistic meaning, however, must be handled by linguists.

The last few pages have been devoted to some kinds of linguistic structure, that is, the synthesis of linguistic elements by the speaker and the corresponding analysis of the result by a hearer. We have noted that under certain circumstances the meaning of the Latin accusative case may be represented in English by word order, while the meaning of the Latin dative case may sometimes be represented in English by word order and sometimes by a short word, usually *to* or *for*. Inflectional endings or prefixes, word order, certain short words (sometimes called auxiliaries), and the like constitute the grammatical machinery

8. See Leonard Bloomfield, Tagalog Texts = "University of Illinois Studies in Language and Literature," 3. 146–209 (1917).

9. See Leonard Bloomfield, "Meaning," Monatshefte für deutschen Unterricht, 35. 101–106 (1943).

of languages. The meanings of these elements (functional elements they have been called) of a language necessarily play as large a part in the descriptive grammar of that language as they do in the speaking or understanding of the language. Nevertheless it is often extremely difficult to define their meaning clearly; it is doubtful whether the thing can be done without the liberal use of examples. And the examples alone are enough, provided the reader fully understands these; in any case, the grammar is never fully understood until the examples can stand alone, without translation or explanation.

It is impossible to distinguish sharply between functional meaning and lexical meaning. There is no doubt that in the Latin phrase *puerī pater* or in English *the boy's father,* the words *puerī* and *boy's* both have functional meaning, and that the latter is closely tied up with the case-ending. In *iuvenēs veniunt* or *the boys come* the distinction is not so sharp; the plural number certainly modifies the lexical meaning (cf. such a collective noun as *iuventūs*), but it is precisely the plural number of *iuvenēs* that justifies the plural verb *veniunt* (contrast *iuventūs venit*).

LEXICOGRAPHY [10]

94. The definition or description of word meaning is often as difficult as the definition of functional meaning. Says Bloomfield (p. 139):

> We can define the meaning of a speech-form accurately when this meaning has to do with some matter of which we possess scientific knowledge. We can define the names of minerals, for example, in terms of chemistry and mineralogy, as when we say that the ordinary meaning of the word *salt* is 'sodium chloride (NaCl),' and we can define the names of plants or animals by means of the technical terms of botany and zoölogy, . . .

This is obviously true; a complete and accurate definition of the commonest meaning of English *horse* is the technical term *equus caballus,* because there are scientific treatises that give full descriptions of this genus and species. The addition of a brief non-technical description and a picture solves the problem of the dictionary maker perfectly. Webster's New International says: "a large solid-hoofed, herbivorous mammal (equus caballus), domesticated by man since a prehistoric

10. See reference in note 9.

period, and used as a beast of burden or a draft-animal, or for riding." There is also a picture, and a list of forty-seven external parts, identified by numbers on the picture. This is certainly enough—more than is needed by anyone who has access to an encyclopedia.

95. Much more difficult is the word *whale,* since it applies to animals of several different genera. The feature that is common to *whales* and which marks them off from other animals is their peculiar treatment by man; they are hunted for their oil and whalebone.

The article in the Oxford Dictionary begins:

Whale: 1. Any of the larger fish-like marine mammals of the order *cetacea,* which have fore-limbs like fins and a tail with horizontal flukes, and are hunted for their oil and whalebone. In wider (scientific) use, any cetacean of the groups *Mystoceti,* or whale-bone whales, and *Odontoceti,* or toothed-whales (which are distinguished by the names dolphin, grampus, porpoise, etc.).

The first sentence here is satisfactory, but the second is inconsistent with it, and should form a new paragraph. The difficulty is typical of most attempts to define popular words in scientific language. Any system of meaning involves an analysis of the universe, and of course the analysis that is gradually being made by the sciences is far more thorough and precise than any other. But linguists must deal chiefly with popular language, which is based upon a very different analysis of the universe, the one, namely, that is performed during the life of each speaker.

96. As William James strikingly phrased it:[11]

The baby, assailed by eyes, ears, nose, skin, and entrails at once, feels it all as one great blooming buzzing confusion . . . That confusion is the baby's universe; and the universe of all of us is still to a great extent such a confusion, potentially resolvable, and demanding to be resolved, but not yet actually resolved, into parts.

Of course the earliest stages in the analysis of each baby's universe must be his individual achievement, but more and more he falls under the influence of his elders, and presently all further analysis comes to be motivated and controlled by language; i.e., by the common sense of the surrounding speakers. As we have already noted **(§ 1),** science has

11. This passage is a fusion of similar passages in Principles of Psychology, 1. 488, New York (1890) and Psychology, p. 16, New York (1892).

passed along this same road, but common sense and popular language lag so far behind that they must generally be treated separately.

The physicist's definition of the word *thunder* will identify the phenomenon—for a physicist. Webster's New International says: "The sound which follows a flash of lightning, due to the sudden expansion of the air in the path of the discharge." This is quite irrelevant for the child, who is frightened and runs to his mother's arms; it is equally irrelevant for the poet who uses the word as a metaphor, and also, I think, for my understanding of the English language. It must be admitted that the child, the poet, and I will not apply to the dictionary for any explanation of our emotional reactions. Whoever does consult the dictionary will want a clear identification of the word's primary meaning, and that he will get.

For many meanings science is of scarcely any help at all. American English *bug* applies to any small animal or to bacteria in a vaguely depreciatory way. It always suggests an insect, but even bacteriologists, in conversation, use it of microscopic plants. To list all the genera and species to which the word has been applied would not be worth while, since it might tomorrow be applied to another one with equal propriety.

If anyone is dealing with a language whose speakers worship the sky as an all-seeing and all-powerful god, it will not help at all to discuss the moisture in the atmosphere and its refraction of light, which makes men seem to see a vault above the earth. The lexicographer must describe the sky god whom the speakers worship. Again, if a community believes in free will, the linguist must, within certain limits, speak as if he also accepted that doctrine.

97. Such words as *love* and *hate* set an impossible task for the lexicographer. Probably his best recourse is to cite a long list of passages in which the word is used, carefully classifying them to bring out the different usages. This could be supplemented by a list of synonyms, and an attempt to differentiate between them.

The difficulty, however, belongs chiefly to the lexicographer. The words *love* and *hate* are among the most efficient in the English language. They are spoken in very various situations, and therefore must vary considerably in meaning; but for all that, they are readily understood by all hearers. Furthermore, many, if not all, languages provide roughly equivalent pairs of terms that have similarly drastic effects under appropriate circumstances. Most remarkable of all, we have observed that to some extent men can understand the mating calls and the cries of rage of other animals (§ 69).

VARIATION IN LEXICAL CATEGORIES

98. Somewhat analogous to structural differences between languages are the incongruities in word meaning. If an animal or plant or other object serves about the same function in the life of several communities, the languages spoken in those communities may show nearly a one to one correspondence in their words for such objects. English *horse* in its commonest meaning can be rather neatly translated by Greek *hippos,* Latin *equos,* French *cheval,* German *Pferd,* etc., and English *dog* corresponds pretty well to Greek *cyōn,* Latin *canis,* French *chien,* German *Hund,* etc. Of course most languages have synonyms for these words, such as English *pony, nag, steed,* Greek *celēs,* Latin *caballus, mannus,* German *Ross,* and the distinctions between the synonyms do not correspond from language to language.

Very frequently we find a more serious incongruity; Latin *altus* represents English *deep* as well as *high,* although the distinction can be made by the less frequent and more formal words *excelsus* 'high' and *profundus* 'deep.'

STYLISTIC

99. Stylistic treats of a selection among the linguistic forms described by grammar and lexicography. This selection depends in part upon the social level of the speaker, and is closely analogous to the local differences that were mentioned in §§ 49 and 50.

For the most part stylistic treats of the artistic modification of speech for aesthetic purposes or for the sake of securing a particular effect. Since this book is devoted to science rather than to art, we must leave the prescription of rules for the effective use of language to treatises on rhetoric, and the description of the style of particular authors to essays on those authors.

The Geneva School of linguists has paid much attention to stylistic; we may mention Charles Bally, Le langage et la vie, 2d ed. Paris (1926), which contains references to earlier work.

CHAPTER VII

THE EMPIRICAL BASIS OF PHONETIC LAWS

100. It has been observed that many words which had the accented vowel *ā* in Old English appear in Modern English with [ow]; in the following typical examples the modern words all contain the same vowel phoneme in spite of their various spelling.

Old English	Modern English	Old English	Modern English
āþ	*oath*	*hām*	*home*
āgan	*own*	*mān*	*moan*
bān	*bone*	*rād*	*road*
bāt	*boat*	*sāwan*	*sow*
gāt	*goat*	*stān*	*stone*
fām	*foam*	*tācen*	*token*
hāl	*whole*		

Since Old English is an earlier stage of Modern English, these correspondences are conveniently summarized in the formula: Old English accented *ā* has become Modern English [ow]. Such a formula is commonly known as a **phonetic law.**

101. Similar sets of correspondences can always be observed, not only between two chronological stages of a language, but also between related languages. We illustrate with the initial consonants of the following pairs of English and German words. In most of these instances the meaning of the two members of the pair is identical or nearly so; the differing meaning of several German words is noted.

English	German	English	German
tail	*Zagel*	*tap*	*Zapfen* 'peg'
tale	*Zahl* 'number'	*tear*	*zehren*
tame	*zahm*	*ten*	*zehn*

English	German	English	German
timber	*Zimmer* 'room'	*tooth*	*Zahn*
tin	*Zinn*	*twelve*	*zwölf*
to, too	*zu*	*twenty*	*zwanzig*
toe	*Zehe*	*twist*	*Zwist* 'quarrel'
token	*Zeichen*	*twitch*	*zwicken*
tongs	*Zange*	*twitter*	*zwitschern*
tongue	*Zunge*	*two*	*zwei*

Here our formula (phonetic law) may be: English initial *t* corresponds to German initial *z*.[1] Since, however, these two West Germanic languages are known to be modern forms of a single prehistoric language, conventionally named **Proto-West Germanic,**[2] it is possible to state the correspondence from the historical point of view: Proto-West Germanic initial *t* remains in English but becomes German *z*.

102. Not infrequently a regular phonetic change operates in such a way as to split a single phoneme into two or more. For example the Latin phoneme *c* [k] has yielded the three phonemes [k], [s], and [š] of Modern French. The following pairs are typical.

Latin	French
cor	*coeur* 'heart'
clāvis	*clef* 'key'
clārus	*clair* 'clear'
crēdere	*croire* 'believe'
cornū	*cor* 'horn'
collus	*cou* 'neck'
coquere	*cuire* 'cook'
cubitus	*coude* 'elbow'

The phonetic law is: Latin *c* [k] before a back vowel (*o* or *u*) or a consonant remains [k] in Modern French.

In spite of the change of Latin [k] to [s] in certain words the writing with the letter *c* has remained unchanged.

1. The correspondence between English *t* and German *z* is not confined to the initial position, but we have given evidence for that position only.

2. The method of reconstructing a prehistoric language from its surviving descendents will be discussed in Chapter XV.

Latin	French
centum	*cent* 'hundred'
cervus	*cerf* 'stag'
cēra	*cire* 'wax'
cessāre	*cesser* 'cease'
cinis	*cendre* 'ashes'
cīnctūra	*ceinture* 'girdle'
cīvitās	*cité* 'city'

The phonetic law is: Latin *c* [k] before *e* or *i*, long or short, becomes Modern French [s].

In those words in which Latin *c* has now come to be pronounced [š], the modern spelling is *ch*.

Latin	French
cantāre	*chanter* 'sing'
carbō	*charbon* 'charcoal'
campus	*champ* 'field'
cārus	*cher* 'dear'
capillus	*cheveu* 'hair'
caballus	*cheval* 'horse'
causa	*chose* 'affair'
caulis	*chou* 'cabbage'

The phonetic law is: Latin *c* [k] before *a*, long or short, becomes Modern French [š].

German loans from Old French preserve an intermediate stage between Latin *c* [k] before *ĕ̄* or *ĭ̄* and Modern French [s]. German *Zeder* 'cedar' was borrowed from Old French *cedre* when *c* was pronounced [ts]. Just so German *Zisterne* 'cistern,' *Zirkel* 'circle,' and *zentral* 'central' preserve the [ts] of Old French *cisterne, cercle, central.* Since the Germans learned Latin from French schoolmasters at a time when *c* before original *ĕ̄* or *ĭ̄* stood for [ts], Latin words such as *centrum* and *Cicerō* were pronounced with [ts] by teachers and pupils, and so they are to this day in Germany.

Similarly Old French *c* from Latin *c* before *ă̄* represented the pronunciation [č], as we learn from mediaeval English loans; for that pronunciation still survives. Examples are:

Latin	Old French	English
catēna	*chaeine*	*chain*
cathedra	*chaiere*	*chair*
camera	*chambre*	*chamber*
cantāre	*chanter*	*chant*

With these words we may contrast English loans from Modern French, such as *chauffeur, chef, chemise, chic.*

103. 1. Frequently the record is less simple and clear than it is in the above instances; there may be a very considerable **residue** of forms which do not accord with any phonetic law that can be formulated. Further study has again and again yielded a satisfactory account of all or nearly all these aberrant forms. A typical example is the prehistoric change of **Proto-Indo-European** [3] intervocalic *s* to Latin *r*. Evidence for the original sibilant is sometimes found in related Latin forms in which the *s* is initial or final or next a consonant, and very frequently we find evidence for it in the related languages. Here are a few examples:

nefās 'wickedness'	*nefārius* 'wicked'
ustus 'burnt'	*ūrere* 'burn'
questus 'complaint'	*querī* 'complain'
flōs 'flower'	*flōris* (genitive)
genus 'race'	*generis* (genitive)
arbos [4] 'tree'	*arboris* (genitive)
Lases [4] tutelary gods	*Larēs*
melius 'better' (neuter singular)	*meliōris* (genitive)
est, sunt [5] 'is, are'	*erit* (future)

Praenestine [6]	*Numasioi*	*Numeriō* (personal name)
Paelignian [6]	*coisatens*	*cūrāvērunt* 'they cared for'
Gothic	*swistar* [7]	*soror* 'sister'
Old English	*sweostor* [7]	

3. The languages related to English, German, Swedish, Russian, Greek, Latin, Sanskrit, etc., are known as the *Indo-European Languages.* The prehistoric language from which they are all descended is called Proto-Indo-European (§ 224).

4. *Arbos* and *Lases* are Early Latin forms.

5. The root of this verb is (*e*)*s*-; the future was formerly *es-e-t.*

6. These are ancient dialects of Italy, closely related to Latin.

7. The -*t*- of Gothic and English developed between *s* and *r* in prehistoric Germanic.

Sanskrit	*janasas*	*generis* 'of a race'
Greek	*geneos* [8]	
Sanskrit	*tāsām*	*istārum* (genitive plural feminine of pronouns)
Greek	*tāōn*	

103. 2. Such forms as *melior* beside neuter *melius* and classical *arbor* in place of earlier *arbos* evidently represent a spread of *r* from the position between vowels in *meliōris, arboris,* etc.; they are said to be analogical forms, and will be discussed in Chapter X. Just so, *s* has occasionally spread from a position where it is normal into the intervocalic position where *r* would be expected; *situs* 'placed' has induced *s* in the compound *po-situs,* and *sī* 'if' is the source of *s* in *nisi* 'if not.'

103. 3. There remain many instances of *s* between vowels in Latin; these originated in various ways. It is clear that long *s* (written *ss*) escaped the change to *r.* Thus we have imperfect subjunctive *essem* beside imperfect indicative *eram* and future indicative *erō,* and *ss* from dental plus *t* remains in many participles like *sessus* 'seated' (from **sed-tus*), *missus* 'sent' (from **mit-tus*). Around the beginning of the Christian era long *s* was shortened after a long vowel or diphthong, when we have such words as *dīvīsus* 'divided' beside *dīvidō, caesus* 'cut' beside *caedō, causa* 'cause' from early Latin *caussa, mīsī* 'I sent' from **mīssī* (root *mit-* plus *-sī*).

103. 4. In *miser* 'wretched' and *caesariēs* 'mane' *s* between vowels is followed by intervocalic *r* in the next syllable, and it has been suggested that the retention of the sibilant may be due to the dissimilative effect of that phoneme.[9]

103. 5. Many instances of *s* between vowels in Latin occur in loan words such as Greek *philosophus, basis, genesis,* or dialectic Italic *amāsius* 'lover.'[10] The lack of etymological connections, either in Latin itself or in the related languages, for the common words *asinus* 'ass,' *casa* 'house,' and *rosa* 'rose' suggests that they also are loan words, although their source is unknown.

103. 6. It is clear from a study of the above material that the change

8. In Greek *s* between vowels was lost.

9. Cf. Chapter IX, §§ 134, 135. We cannot suppose that *miser* and *caesariēs* changed to *mirer* and *caerariēs* and then suffered dissimilation, because inherited *r . . . r* remains in *marmor, mīror, mīrārī,* etc. On *caesariēs,* see Ernout-Meillet, s.v.

10. See A. Ernout, Les éléments dialectaux du vocabulaire latin, p. 104, Paris (1909).

of intervocalic *s* to *r* was completed before our earliest records of urban Latin; Praenestine *Numasioi* of the seventh or sixth century B.C. is not evidence for the language of Rome. After the completion of the change *s* came to stand between vowels in Latin in various ways, and it remained unchanged. When allowance is made for a known phonetic law (*ss* became *s* after long vowels and diphthongs), analogical changes (e.g., *positus, nisi*), and certain or probable loans, there remain only a very few unexplained forms such as *miser* and *caesariēs,* and even for these a plausible guess can be made.

104. We have seen that with remarkable consistency Old English accented *ā* becomes Modern English [ow]; Modern English initial *t* corresponds to German *z;* Latin *c* before back vowels or consonants remains in French as [k]; Latin *c* before *ĕ̄* and *ī* becomes Old French [ts] and Modern [s]; Latin *c* before *ă̄* becomes Old French [č] and Modern [š]; Proto-Indo-European intervocalic *s* becomes Latin *r.*

These regular correspondences of sounds attracted the attention of scholars from the earliest days of the science, but it was not at first apparent that they were anything essentially different from the aberrant cases. In Latin, it was thought, original intervocalic *s* became *r* in most words, but remained in *positus, nisi, miser, caesariēs, causa,* and many other words. Original final *s* might remain unchanged, as in *genus, melius, nefās, es,* etc., or it might become *r* as in *arbor, melior, dēgener,* etc. Gradually more and more of the apparent exceptions were explained, until so few were left that the conclusion seemed inevitable that, if we had complete knowledge, they also would find their explanation.

In the 1870's a number of scholars announced, somewhat dogmatically, that phonetic laws have no exceptions. The earliest declaration of this sort seems to have been made by August Leskein [11] in 1876, but the discovery really belonged to a group, who, from that time to this, have been called the neo-grammarians (*Junggrammatiker*). The neogrammarians aroused some opposition from their older contemporaries on the ground that they were going too far, that they were elevating into a hard and fast principle what might better be called a tendency. We must emphasize, however, that they did not break with the past

11. Die Deklination im Slavisch-Litauischen und Germanischen, pp. xxviii and 1. Leipzig (1876).

of the science; the opposition between the two groups soon resolved itself into a discussion about generalizations, while all treated most matters of detail in the same way; the regular operation of the phonetic laws was taken for granted by all competent scholars, unless some specific analogical or other explanation of an apparent exception could be pointed out.

105. As an illustration of the clarity that careful observation of the phonetic laws can bring into comparative grammar we may consider the endings of the accusative singular of Greek and Latin nouns and adjectives.

o-stems	*i*-stems	*u*-stems	cons. stems
anthrōpo-n 'man'	*poli-n* 'city'	*hēdy-n* [12] 'sweet'	*pod-a* 'foot'
servo-m 'slave'	*tussi-m* 'cough'	*exercitu-m* 'army'	*ped-em* 'foot'

In both languages a final nasal appears after the stem of nouns whose stem ends in a vowel (other considerations combine to indicate that original final *m* becomes Greek *n*). In Latin the consonant-stem accusative *pedem* also has a final nasal, but there is no nasal in Greek *poda.* There is a similar anomaly in the negative prefix, Sanskrit *a-,* Greek *a-,* Latin *in-,* Germanic *un-*. There are many other Greek words, and also Sanskrit words, which show *a* where we might expect a nasal, e.g., Greek *epathon* 'I suffered' beside perfect *催pepontha;* Greek *deca,* Sanskrit *daça* beside Latin *decem,* Gothic *taíhun* 'ten'; Greek *he-caton,* Sanskrit *çatam* beside Latin *centum,* Gothic *hund* 'hundred.' All these words find their explanation in the phonetic law: original syllabic *m̩* and *n̩* become Greek *a,* Sanskrit *a,* Latin *em, en,*[13] Germanic *um, un.*

After this it is easy to understand the similar difficulty in the Greek accusative plural, masculine and feminine, of the consonant stems. Forms in the related languages show that the long vowels before final *s* in Greek *anthrōpous, polīs, hēdȳs* and in Latin *servōs, tussīs,* and *exercitūs* are due to lengthening upon loss of *n* before *s;* the original case-ending was *-ns.* If a consonant preceded, as in the word for 'foot,' the nasal was syllabic *n̩* (like *en* in English *fatten*) instead of consonantal *n;* Proto-Indo-European *ped-n̩s* yielded prehistoric Latin *ped-ens,*

12. Proto-Indo-European *u* became Greek *y.*

13. The Latin negative prefix *in-* has undergone a further change of Early Latin initial *en-* to *in-*.

whence *ped-ēs;* but Proto-Indo-European *pod-n̥s* yielded Greek *pod-as* (without nasal and therefore without subsequent lengthening of *a*).

106. At least equally important is the help gained from the phonetic laws in eliminating false etymologies. It seemed obvious to the early comparatists that Greek *theos* 'god' and Latin *deus* 'god' must be identified. The one apparent difficulty was presented by the initial consonants; Greek initial *th* corresponds to Latin *f* in *thēk̨e* 'placed' beside Latin *fēcit* 'made,' Greek *thūmos* 'spirit, courage' beside Latin *fūmus* 'smoke, vapor,' and in other words, while Latin *d* corresponds to Greek *d* in Latin *dare* Greek *dounai* 'to give,' Latin *duo* Greek *dyō* 'two,' Latin *edere* Greek *edmenai* 'to eat,' Latin *vidēre* Greek *idein* 'to see.' Nevertheless there are a few pairs in which Latin *d* corresponds to Greek *th* (Latin *con-dere* Greek *syn-theinai* 'put together,' Latin *viduos* Greek *ēitheos* 'unmarried'); and so it was customary to hold that original *dh* might appear in Latin either as *f* or as *d*. We now understand that the latter development occurs only in the interior of a word between vowels and after *n*. Therefore *theos* and *deus* cannot be cognate words.

Confirmation of this conclusion comes from both languages. (a) Greek *thes-phatos* 'spoken, decreed by god' and several other compounds with initial *thes-* must contain the word for 'god'; an earlier stage of *theos* was evidently *thesos,* which regularly lost *s* between *vowels* (see above, n. 8). But we have seen that in Latin *s* between vowels must appear as *r*. (b) Latin *deus* is a by-form of *dīvus* from Proto-Indo-European *deiwos* 'heavenly, god,' whence Sanskrit *devas* 'god.'[14]

107. For a similar reason French *grotte* 'crypt' cannot be derived from Latin *crupta,* since this would yield French **croute*.[15] Latin *crupta,* however, regularly became Italian *grotta,* and when Italian nouns are borrowed by French, final *-a* becomes mute *e*.

108. The regularity of phonetic change—the validity of the phonetic laws—is a doctrine based upon observation. It was arrived at with much reluctance, and only after other hypotheses had been found unsatisfactory. This doctrine is now accepted by linguists simply because it works.

14. Proto-Italic *deivos* became Early Latin *dēus* (with *ē* more like *ī* than the inherited *ē* of *fēcit*), and shortening of the long vowel before another vowel gave *deus*. On the other hand, genitive *deivī* regularly yielded *dīvī*. Analogy filled out both declensions, and the meanings were slightly differentiated.

15. The actual French *croûte* 'crust' is from Latin *crusta*.

In other words, it is like all other scientific generalizations in that it is subject to change as soon as anyone can state a generalization that will fit the facts better.

This empirical generalization, of course, is all we need to carry on the work of historical linguistics. We shall see in Chapter XV that the entire structure of comparative grammar is founded upon the hypothesis of the regularity of phonetic change. It follows that if the hypothesis proves unsound, the structure must fall to the ground. Therefore the complexity combined with the plausibility of comparative grammar as we know it goes far toward guaranteeing the truth of the underlying hypothesis. It is almost as certain as the geographer's working hypothesis that the earth is round.[16]

16. Someone will rise to say that the earth is not round but spheroidal. In the next chapter we shall have occasion to suggest that some phonetic changes may not be regular.

CHAPTER VIII

WHY ARE PHONETIC LAWS REGULAR?

109. In Chapter VII we have passed in review a few of the changes of sound in the history of various languages, and we have noted that they can be satisfactorily described by formulas of the type: phoneme *a* of an earlier stage of a language becomes phoneme *b* of a later stage. Such a formula, or phonetic law, must sometimes include a limiting phrase such as "if accented" or "before front vowels" or "if an aspirate follows in the next syllable." Scholars have discovered that in all languages yet studied the phonetic laws, if carefully stated, are extraordinarily regular.

110. In some cases there is no doubt what makes them regular. If an adult learns a new language he almost always substitutes for some of its phonemes the most similar phonemes of his native language. Many Germans speak English with the German uvular *r,* and many Frenchmen substitute the tense [i] of French for the lax [ɪ] of English *pin;* in both cases they do this with complete regularity. In the conditions prevailing in the United States many foreigners continue to employ these regular sound-substitutions as long as they live; but their children usually, and their grandchildren almost always, discard them. There is little chance for the numerous imported languages spoken here permanently to change the phonemes of American English.

If, however, a community learns a foreign language from conquerors or tradesmen, and if the learners outnumber the model speakers, the complete mastery of the foreign phonemes may be indefinitely delayed. If the supply of speakers of the intruding language is not constantly renewed some phonemic features of the original language may survive. Something like this may have happened in various parts of the Roman Empire, but proof is not available. The [y] of French for Latin [u·], as in *mur* 'wall' from Latin *mūrus,* may contain a Gaulish phoneme, if indeed ancient Gaulish had this phoneme.

A better documented instance is the retention of the French type of accent (on all syllables without much difference) in the Alemannic

German dialects which were introduced into southwestern Switzerland during the Middle Ages. This accentuation protected the final vowels which were unaccented and therefore lost in other High German dialects.[1]

An earlier language that has thus bequeathed one or more linguistic features to a successor language is sometimes called the linguistic substratum. Features surviving from a linguistic substratum are extremely difficult to identify with certainty.

111. Ever since the appearance of Paul's Prinzipien [2] in 1880, many linguists have ascribed the regularity of phonetic changes to gradual and harmonious development within a linguistic community. Thus Leonard Bloomfield [3] writes:

> Historically we picture phonetic change as a gradual favoring of some non-distinctive [i.e., meaningless] variants [i.e., allophones] and the disfavoring of others. It could be observed only by means of an enormous mass of mechanical records, reaching through several generations of speakers.

Paul regarded the gradualness of the change as an essential factor in its regularity; any noticeable variation would provoke correction. Paul held that the favoring of certain variants must be sought in the nature of the speech organs of the linguistic community.

This theory is obviously incapable of proof, but it is given a certain plausibility by the intermediate stages that are often recorded in one way or another during the history of a phonetic change. We have noticed, for example, that Latin *c* before *e* and *i* has developed into French [s] by way of Old French [ts] (see § **102**). Between Proto-Germanic [ai] (evidenced, for example, by Gothic *stains* 'stone' and *aiþs* 'oath') and Modern English [ow] in *stone, oath* (see § **100**), we can establish Old English [a·], Middle English [ɔ·], and Early Modern English [o·].[4]

The difficulty with the theory is that we can rarely find any cause that should lead to a "gradual favoring of some non-distinctive features and disfavoring of others," and until some such factor can be pointed out

1. Wm. Moulton, Swiss German Dialect and Romance Patois = Language Dissertations, 34 (1941).

2. Hermann Paul, Prinzipien der Sprachgeschichte, Halle (1880; 5th ed. 1920). Chapter 3 treats of "Change of Sound."

3. Language, p. 365.

4. See Jespersen, Modern English Grammar 1. 231 f., 244.

we must expect the several meaningless variants to cancel out; marksmen will, in general, distribute their hits pretty evenly about the bull's eye unless some defect in the gun or in the bow and arrow leads to a consistent error in aim. Occasionally, to be sure, some factor in a given speech community may act upon all its members so as to deflect their pronunciation in a given direction. I wrote as follows in 1917:[5]

> The weakening of unaccented *a* was induced by the strong stress-accent of early Latin, an influence that must constantly have affected all speakers. Every time any one pronounced a word like **réfaciō* he tended to make the second vowel a little closer and less sonorous than before; the change, however, was very slight in each case and therefore did not attract attention or provoke correction. Nevertheless each new stage on the road from *a* to *i* must have served as a point of departure for another change in the same direction.

All this is true if the initial accent of prehistoric Latin was really the efficient cause of the change and not merely a limiting condition. While the gradualness of a change may, under some circumstances, help to make it regular, we have still to explain in all such cases why there should be any change at all.

112. There are, besides, many regular phonetic changes which cannot go forward by imperceptible degrees. There are scarcely any better established phonetic laws than those which describe the dissimilation of aspirates in Indic and Greek, and yet Brugmann is certainly right in classifying such changes as sudden (*springender Lautwandel*). Since Greek, for example, possessed the phoneme *t* beside the phoneme *th*, a succession of phonemes *th* . . . *th* could not gradually change to *t* . . . *th;* each occurrence of the first phoneme in such a word as *thithēmi* must belong either to the *th* phoneme or to the *t* phoneme. To put it more concretely, if the first *th* gradually lost its aspiration, a time would come when some instances of it would differ too much from the second *th* to be accepted, by hearer and speaker, as allophones of the same phoneme; they would rather be understood as allophones of the phoneme *t*. Whereupon either a correction would be made, or the remainder of the dissimilation would be completed at once. It is for this reason that many scholars have maintained that no regularity is to be expected in dissimilative and assimilative changes.[6]

5. Linguistic Change, p. 78.
6. Such changes will be discussed in Chapter IX, §§ 128–135.

113. A phonetic innovation that cannot arise by a series of minimal changes cannot be a communal product; any sudden change must start from a single speaker or from several speakers independently, and, just so, it must start in a single word or in several words independently. If it comes to be adopted by the community, it must somehow spread from speaker to speaker and from word to word.

114. Even some phonetic innovations that may have arisen by a series of minimal changes are known to have spread by some kind of secondary process—some sort of borrowing. The phoneme *h* was completely lost in several Greek dialects, including Eastern Ionic, before the date of our earliest records. In Attic and Hellenistic Greek, however, the phoneme was preserved until after the beginning of the Christian era.[7] Since Modern Greek, which comes from Hellenistic Greek, preserves no trace of a phoneme *h,* we must assume either that the sound was lost independently in Hellenistic Greek or that the lack of it spread to that dialect from one or more of those that lacked it in ancient times.

115. The High German change of *k̨* to *ch,* whence *ich* and *machen* as against Low German *ik̨* and *mak̨en,* has been carried through with great regularity in most of the area in which it appears at all; but along the dividing line between the two areas there is some disagreement between words and between speakers. Thus in Düsseldorf the same speakers say *ich* but *mak̨en.*[8]

116. At some time in the Middle Ages, Proto-West-Germanic *ū* in such words as *hūs* 'house' and *mūs* 'mouse' became [y·], i.e., French *u,* in the Netherlands. The change spread toward the east, encroaching more and more upon the territory of Low German [hu·s] and [mu·s]. The standard Dutch [hy·s] spread farther than the homely word [my·s], and so there is a considerable area in eastern Holland where [hy·s] and [mu·s] are spoken side by side. Several later changes have eliminated both [hy·s] and [my·s] from large regions, but there is today some inconsistency between the words [hy·s] and [mu·s] in the east.[9]

7. Sturtevant, Pronunciation, 2d ed. pp. 69–73.

8. See § 50 and Figure 2.

9. For details see G. G. Kloeke, De Hollandsche Expansie, The Hague (1927), or the review of this by Leonard Bloomfield, Language, 4. 284–288 (1928). The most important points are summarized in Bloomfield's Language, pp. 328–331.

117. Many years ago Moritz Trautmann[10] published an account of the origin of uvular *r* in Paris in the seventeenth century and of its spread through the large cities of France and then through many regions of Germany. The story as he tells it is certainly incomplete; Basilius shows that the sound was brought to Berlin by Huguenots, who became teachers in the schools. There is, however, no reason to doubt Trautmann's account of his own experiences of the rivalry of tongue-tip *r* and uvular *r*. He says (p. 220):

When I attended the gymnasium in Eisleben, all the older people still spoke a tongue-tip *r*, but against my school-mates I often had to defend my own tongue-tip *r* with my fists. In Eisleben, during my student years in Halle and Berlin, and just so during the last six years in Leipzig, I have many times observed that persons newly arrived from the country, students, maids, house-servants, store-clerks, find no task more urgent than to rid themselves of their excellent tip-tongue *r* and to growl with a uvular *r*.

Dr. Emil Froeschels, formerly of Vienna, said in a talk before the Linguistic Institute in Ann Arbor, on July 10, 1940, that in recent years the tongue-tip *r*, which has always remained in many rural districts, has been coming back into fashion in the city of Vienna.

118. Most of the phonetic changes recorded in our historical grammars cover such wide areas that we must probably assume a considerable spread from their points of origin.[11] Since all perceptible phonetic innovations can occur only in the utterance of particular words by particular speakers, they can spread only by the imitative pronunciation of particular words by one or another hearer. Such a process must necessarily lead to irregularity, i.e., to variations between words and between speakers, such as we have illustrated.

119. Nevertheless there are actual records of vacillation between two rival phonemes ending in the complete victory of one of them. Middle English [wa] has become [wɔ] in British English of the present day except before back consonants and *f*.[12] Jespersen cites Shakespeare's

10. Anglia, 3.212–222 (1880); cf. Basilius, Modern Language Quarterly, 3.449–455 (1942).

11. Cf. J. Vendryes, Language, a Linguistic Introduction to History (translated by Paul Radin), pp. 45–47, New York (1925).

12. Jespersen, Modern English Grammar, 1.317. He records a rare variant of *quaff* with [ɔ], and The Oxford Dictionary gives only [ɔ] for *waffle;* the latter word, however, originated in America, and probably [ɔ] in both words is of American origin.

rimes (*watch : match; wanting : granting; war : afar, bar, scar; warm : harm*) as evidence for persistence of the old [wa] in his time. Jespersen finds the earliest mention of the rounded vowel after *w* in 1640, but he continues:

The old unrounded sound seems to have survived till the end of the eighteenth century as an occasional or individual pronunciation; Enfield (1790) gives *wash,* etc., in his own pronunciation as equal to the vowel of *hat,* and *water, wart, dwarf* with the vowel of *half, ass,* while Walker (1791) says that 'we frequently hear' *quality* with the vowel of *legality* instead of that of *jollity.*

The English language was brought to America during the two centuries of vacillation between [wa] and [wɔ], and among us that vacillation still persists. I have heard from American speakers of standard English both [a] and [ɔ] in the words *warm, want, water, wash, watch, quality, wad, wabble, waffle,* and *wallop.* Some of us [waš] in [wɔtr], while others [waš] in [watr] and others still, like the British, [wɔš] in [wɔtr]; a few Americans [wɔš] in [watr].

119a. Materials collected for the Linguistic Atlas of the United States and Canada indicate that in a part of western Pennsylvania the inherited phonemes [a] and [ɔ] have been completely fused, both in the *wa*-words and in all others. How far west of the Ohio boundary this state of affairs extends is not now known.

120. Very instructive is Jespersen's [13] account of [kj, gj] for [k, g] in such words as *can, cow, get, begin,* pronunciations that were more or less fashionable in the seventeenth and eighteenth centuries but that gradually died out in the nineteenth. In American English also [kj, gj] had a considerable vogue in some regions, but lost prestige during the nineteenth century. In this case, then, the net result of years of vacillation between an older and a newer rival has been the actual or imminent victory of the older.

121. Similarly in Latin of the last century B.C. such forms as *pulcher, triumphus,* and *Carthāgō,* with imitation of *ch, ph,* and *th* in loanwords from the Greek, became so fashionable,[14] that Cicero, who knew that *ch, ph,* and *th* had no business in Latin, confessed to using them in these words. No trace of the fashion survives in the Romance lan-

13. Modern English Grammar, 1. 349 f.
14. Sturtevant, Pronunciation, 2d ed. pp. 158–160.

guages, and even Quintilian, who died in 95 A.D., says that he has seen on inscriptions such forms as *choronae* and *chenturiones* but does not say that he had himself heard aspirated stops. Gellius, who died 175 A.D., definitely ascribes these phonemes to the "ancients."

122. We must conclude, then, that some of the phonemic changes recorded in our grammars have passed through periods of vacillation, because they could start only by sudden changes in specific words. Other phonemic changes have covered so wide a territory that we must assume periods of spread from speaker to speaker, and this could occur only in connection with the imitation of particular words. Finally we have actual record of periods of vacillation between rival phonemes, leading to the complete victory of one or the other. It is clear that we shall not understand the regularity of the phonetic laws until we learn how rivalry beween phonemes leads to the victory of one of them.

123. Benjamin Ide Wheeler [15] has suggested a way in which the spread of a phonemic feature from speaker to speaker can induce a spread from word to word. He says that in his native dialect he pronounced *new* and *Tuesday* [nu·, tu·zdi], but that he learned to say instead [nju·, tju·zdi]. Sometimes, "when in a mood of uttermost precision," he has caught himself creating such forms as [dju·, tju·] for *do* and *two*.

Such "over-corrections" have been observed very often in many languages. In the Palatinate the *ich*-sound of High German has become [š], and the late Dr. Eva Fiesel is authority for the statement that some natives of this region, when they master the standard pronunciation [iç] for *ich*, say also [kine·ziç, italie·niç, gri·çiç, hypç], etc., for *kinesisch, italienisch, griechisch, hübsch,* etc., in which final [š] is standard.

The Berlin change of standard German *g* to *j* (as in *eine jute jebratene Jans ist eine jute Jabe Jottes*) induces some, who have learned to say *g* in such words, to change *jetzt* and *Jahr* to *getzt* and *Gahr*.

In central New England the struggle between general American *r* before a consonant and the Eastern weakening or loss of *r* in this position has been going on for centuries. It is surely in villages where the Western *r* before a consonant was at the moment gaining ground that the hyper-correct forms [karm] for *calm,* [pɔrn] for *pawn,* and [garglz]

15. Transactions of the American Philological Association, 32. 5–15 (1901, published 1902).

for *goggles*[16] originated. Similarly the imitation of speakers who pronounced *aunt* as [ant] and *dance* as [dans] has led those whose native dialect had [ænt] and [dæns] to say [hand] and [fansi], although their models would have said [hænd] and [fænsi].

A couple who spoke a Western *r* before consonants moved to Eastern New England, and their little daughter promptly learned that her playmates said [jad] where her parents said [jard]. Presently she picked up from the playmates some interesting stories about a giant whom her elders had neglected to tell her of. She reported the giant's name to her parents as [gard].

124. Before a phoneme can spread from word to word in this way it is necessary that one of the two rivals shall acquire some sort of prestige. Most commonly, or at least in most of the recorded cases, it is a standard dialect that causes one phoneme to be preferred to another, but the same thing can happen wherever one local dialect or dialect feature is spreading at the expense of another. In the course of time the balance between the dialects may change, or, for some reason lying outside of the linguistic situation (the rise of a new king or political leader, new trading practices, the introduction of the telephone or the radio), the trend of fashion may change, and so a complicated set of rival forms may interact over a more or less wide territory.

Such is the conflict in American English between [u] and [ʊ][17] in such words as *soot, coop, roof, proof, soon, spoon, broom, room,* and *food.*[18] As far as I know, the confusion does not exist in American English in *fool* and *moon,* which always have [u], or in *good, foot,* and *book,* which always have [ʊ]. How this vacillation started I cannot say, but here and now it is propagated in the way suggested by Wheeler. In my native dialect six of the words in the list (*soot, coop, roof, soon, broom,* and *room*) had [ʊ], but for years I have tended to substitute [u] in all of them.

Another pair of rival phonemes is [i] and [ə] in unaccented final position. In early American English and in local (especially rural) dialects to this day such words as *America, Carolina, China, Florida, Martha,*

16. Reported by Robert J. Menner, American Speech, 12. 168 (1937).

17. For the somewhat different situation in British English, see Jespersen, Modern English Grammar, 1. 334 f.

18. The phoneme [ʊ] is rarer in this word than in others in the list, but it occurs in New England, New York, and Canada.

Rebecca, Sarah, Savannah, sofa, taffeta have final [i]. Since the beginning of the nineteenth century this widespread pronunciation has been condemned and ridiculed; hundreds of Americans have tried to eliminate it from their speech. It would be very strange indeed if some of them had not gone too far and substituted [ə] for [i] in words where the latter had always been at home. As a matter of fact, many Americans speak final [ə] in *Cincinnati, Miami, Missouri, prairie, doily, Dorothy,* and some even in *macaroni* and *spaghetti.* Many, probably most, of the speakers who use these forms learned them from their elders in the ordinary way; but it is difficult to avoid the conclusion that an important factor in their origin was over-correction. Even if, as has been suggested, the change of final [i] to [ə] is connected with the prevalence, in the position before a final consonant, of the reduced vowel [ə] in place of [i] west of the Mississippi, it is still probable that at least *Dorotha* (reported from Pennsylvania), *Cincinnata* and *Miama* (in Ohio), and also *macarona* and *spaghetta* are, in origin, instances of over-correction.[19]

125. It is therefore clear that when a phonemic innovation spreads from speaker to speaker it may tend also to spread from word to word. Even if changes of fashion induce more or less complicated cross influences, there are clear cases of a period of vacillation followed by the victory of one of the rival phonemes. It is probable that the vacillation, once it has started, must ordinarily continue until just this happens, unless some independent force interferes. Among the forces that may do this are the several factors of primary phonetic change (Chapter IX), analogic creation (Chapter X), contamination (Chapter XI), or some conflicting foreign influence in the shape of a new wave of fashion (Chapter XIV).

126. It is here suggested that many—perhaps most—of the phonetic laws recorded in our handbooks describe changes whose regularity is due to dialect mixture. Paradoxically dialect mixture is a familiar explanation of apparent exceptions to the phonetic laws, and there is no doubt of the validity of such explanations in many cases, including several of those just studied. The co-existence of [hy·s] and [mu·s] in east-

19. See Allan Walker Read, American Speech, 8. 422–436 (1933) and references; Robert J. Menner, American Speech, 12. 171 f. (1937).

ern Holland, that of [rum] and [rUm] in American English are both due to dialect mixture; but situations like these tend to be temporary. Social forces, such as the economic law of supply and demand, require time for their operation. Hence it is that we are more likely to find regularity in comparing two chronologically distant stages of a language (e.g., Old English accented *ā* becomes Modern English [ow]) than in studying the dialect geography of an area where intercourse is active (e.g., the pronunciation of *girl* and *oil* in the city of New York).

127. As far as phonetic laws describe phonemic changes that have spread from speaker to speaker and from word to word under the impulse of fashion, some of the dogmatic statements that have frequently been made about them do not apply. We have already noted (**§ 126**) that a regular phonemic change need not occur by imperceptible changes. While it is doubtless true that a change which occurs by imperceptible stages is never observed at the time, there is an excellent chance that speakers will notice a change that is spreading from speaker to speaker and from word to word, as we actually observe our own vacillation between [rum] and [rUm], and as Cicero noticed the vacillation between [pulkher] and [pulker].

Finally, it is impossible to draw a sharp line between the phonetic innovations that spread from word to word while they spread from speaker to speaker and those that confine themselves to one word or a few. An example of the latter class is English [aiðr, naiðr] for *either* and *neither* instead of the older [iðr, niðr]. This innovation does not yet affect any other word than these two, and there is no reason to anticipate that it ever will. But if once the vacillation extends to several other words, such as *eater, preacher,* or *eat, preach, peach,* we may expect the rivalry to continue until [i] or [ai] becomes universal among the words affected. On the other hand, it is conceivable that American English will reach agreement on [ruf, sun, rum], etc., but that [gUd], [fUt], and [bUk] will remain as now. Conversely we may all say [rUf, sUn, rUm] but continue to say [ful] and [mun]. We had better not indulge in generalizations such as "phonetic laws operate without exceptions," but no cautious scholar will claim to have found such an exception unless he is prepared to furnish complete proof. The doctrine of the regularity of phonemic change is firmly based upon a vast amount of careful observation; it cannot be based upon inference from the nature of such change, since there is good reason to believe that phonemic changes can be made regular in several different ways.

CHAPTER IX

ASSIMILATION AND DISSIMILATION

128. Some of the phonetic innovations discussed in Chapter VIII probably or possibly came in from some source outside the linguistic community. The use of the aspirates *ch, ph,* and *th* was introduced into Latin in Greek loan-words such as *chorus, philosophus, theatrum* (cf. § 121 and n. 14). It has been held that the German uvular *r* was imported from France (cf. § 117).

In many other instances the actual rivalry is due to the influence of one local or class dialect upon another (cf. § 126); in the eighteenth century some Americans said *America* and others *Ameriky;* the vacillation discussed above (§ 124) appeared when many speakers shifted from the latter pronunciation to the former.

We have now to consider the origin in a local dialect of phonetic innovations that make possible the sort of rivalry described in Chapter VIII. Our knowledge is here very scanty, and we shall have to confine ourselves to a few topics for which material is especially abundant.

The material occurs in the form of lapses (see above, §§ 56, 57). A significant fact is that certain changes recorded in our historical grammars are closely parallel to these lapses; our classification and our discussion is designed to show the parallelism. In this chapter we shall treat only innovations that belong to the familiar categories of assimilation and dissimilation.

ASSIMILATION

129. As has long been known a phoneme or group of phonemes tends to become similar to or identical with a following phoneme or group of phonemes (Latin *ad* + *petō* > *appetō, in* + *petō* > *impetō*). We shall call this sort of assimilation **anticipation.** Less frequently assimilation is in the reverse direction; a phoneme or group of phonemes becomes similar to or identical with a preceding phoneme or group of phonemes (prehistoric Latin *saldō* : English *salt* > Latin *sallō*). We shall use the term **lag** for this sort of assimilation. The several sub-classes will be clear from their labels.

ANTICIPATION ALONE

130. 1. A speaker intended to say, *the optical illusion,* but actually said, *the illoptical illusion.* He anticipated the initial syllable of the last word and prefixed it to the previous word. We call this anticipation alone in contrast to the next two classes, where something else happens. Another example is *phortograph* for *photograph,* in which the single phoneme *r* is anticipated. I have heard this mispronunciation several times, and it may already have got beyond the status of a lapse; it may be habitual with some speakers. I am sure that this is the case with *ompen* for *open.* Just because this is a habitual pronunciation we cannot be sure of its history; it may come from anticipation of *m* in the common form *opem* [opm], or it may be **onpen* with the customary English partial assimilation of *n* to an immediately following *p.*

Bawden (p. 101) gives an imperfect report of several instances. A speaker intended to say *his face was a play-ground* and he started *his flace—.* Another intended to say *panes of glass* and said *planes;* a third intended *a bright fire blazing* and said *a bright flire.* We are not told whether any of these sentences were completed, or, if so, whether with or without correction by the speaker.

Meringer (pp. 22–37) records a number of examples. We select the following, several of which involve a pause (indicated by three periods) and a following correction. The anticipated phonemes are printed in boldface in each occurrence.

ew**r**ige Nach**r**ichten (for *ewige*)
k**l**aum **l**iegt er
in der St**r**adt d**r**in
Du st**n**udierst [1] **n**icht (for *studierst*)
das unt**l**ere . . . das untere, das dunk**l**ere
der Lehrer**in** . . . Lehrer der Kaiser**in**
Ma**d**rillen . . . Marillen sind schwer ver**d**aulich

Speakers of prehistoric Old High German and Old English apparently anticipated the high front position of the tongue in the vowel of

1. Meringer (p. 30) prints *schtnudierst.*

the plural ending of such words as Old High German *lembir* 'lambs' (from **lambiz*) and Old English *men* (from **manniz*). Hence the vowel *a* of the first syllable was changed to the mid-high, mid-front vowel *e*. Such partial assimilation is more common when the two phonemes are in direct contact (see § **130. 2. 2**).

ANTICIPATION WITH SUBSTITUTION

130. 2. Much more frequently the anticipated matter crowds out a phoneme or group of phonemes and is substituted therefor. In fact this is by far the commonest sort of lapse. We print the anticipated phonemes or groups in boldface, and include the eliminated matter in parentheses, unless a correction by the speaker makes this unnecessary. Such phenomena are frequently classed as distance assimilation and contact assimilation; we shall accordingly separate these two groups.

130. 2. 1. *Distance Anticipation*

Ver(o)**i**nica (a girl's name)
Sy(dn)**l**ey **L**anier
every(th)**h**ing you **h**ear
p(l)**r**aying on the st**r**eet (Bawden, p. 119)
spring (ch)**t**icken **t**en cents a pound (Bawden, p. 117)
shar(p)**f**en the kni**f**e
heroic (c)**p**ouplets
patrio(t)**rt**ic and libe**r**al hea**rt**ed [2]
(s)**sk**ea and **sk**y [2]
on whose (s)**st**ad **st**eps I climb [2]
there is o(ne)**nt** for re**nt** (Bawden, p. 107) [2]
w(a)**o**nn ich k**o**mme
ich muss die Ta(ss)**sch**en wa**sch**en
express**ig**e of . . . expressive of lar**ge** masses

2. These four lapses may possibly be classified under § 130. 1, and printed as follows:
patriortic and liberal hearted
skea and sky
on whose stad steps I climb
there is onet for rent
The chief reason for putting them here is that anticipation alone is so much rarer than anticipation with substitution that it is the less plausible explanation when either is possible. For this reason I have refrained from citing similarly ambiguous material from Meringer's collections.

dafar . . . dafür hast Du aber auch ein Paar sehr gute Schlüsse gemacht
bulliger . . . billiger durch kommen
ich lebe . . . liebe solche Reden
ein hübscher Spiel . . . Stil liegt in ihrer Sprache
Nachbittag . . . Nachmittag bin ich
für jauter . . . lauter Jubiläen
besalters . . . besonders kalte Hände
und strin . . . drin steht

Similar to these lapses are English *four five* and German *vier fünf* in place of the contrasting initials of Indo-European *k̨wetwṓres pénk̨we;* pre-Germanic seems to have changed *hweðwōr* to *feðwōr* by anticipation of the inherited *f* of the next numeral. The initial *ar-* for *ad-* in Latin *arbiter* and *arvorsum* is no doubt due to anticipation of *r* later in the same words. Similarly *arfuisse* reflects anticipation in such forms as *adfuēre, adfueram,* etc. Priscian's *arger* instead of *agger* from **adger* is confirmed by Italian *argine* and Spanish *arcén* 'rampart'; here again *r* comes from the following syllable. Attic Greek substitutes *Orchomenos* for *Erchomenos* in the name of the Boeotian town. Similarly Boeotian *Vhecadāmos* yields Attic *Acadēmos* [3] (with loss of initial *Vh* and change of *ā* to *ē*).

130. 2. 2. *Contact Anticipation*

The results of this process are familiar in many languages; e.g., Latin *accumbō, afficiō, aggerō, allegō, annotō, appetō, arrīdeō, assistō, attrahō* (all with *ad-*), *illicitus, immittō, irrumpō* (with *in-*), etc. One can scarcely doubt that such things as these started in lapses, and it is easy to find similar things in English that have not yet received full recognition in our school grammars. It is hardly ever possible, however, to be certain that we have a lapse rather than a more or less habitual pronunciation. Thus *sidown* for *sit down* is probably the prevailing form, and *nemind* or *nem mind* for *never mind* is almost as common. *A red-hop pok̨er* has a better chance of having been a lapse in the one occurrence reported to me, but I am not sure.

Not infrequently forms current in one language or another show partial assimilation: e.g., Latin *ingerō* [iŋgero·], *imperō* (with *in-*);

3. Schwyzer, Griechische Grammatik, p. 255, lists a number of Greek words that show distance assimilation of vowels, both of this class and of the one treated in § **131.2.**

concurrō [koŋkur·o·], *condōnō, contineō* (with *com-*), *optineō* (with *ob,* or perhaps one should say *obdūcō* with *op-*).[4] In prehistoric Italic *ew* became *ow* by anticipation of the position of lips and tongue required for the consonant; hence Latin *novus* 'new' beside Greek *neos,* earlier *nevos.* A very common pronunciation of English *oat meal* is *oap meal.* Equally familiar is *haf to* for *have to.* Less common, but perhaps scarcely to be called lapses are *dreatful* for *dreadful* and *recodnize* for *recognize. Lenth* for *length* is substandard, but fairly common. In all probability a study of mechanical records containing such words and phrases as *admixture, hot mush, send back* would disclose indubitable lapses illustrating partial assimilation.

ANTICIPATION WITH LOSS

130. 3. The premature utterance of the anticipated phoneme or group of phonemes sometimes inhibits its utterance a second time in its proper place. The result is a change in the position of the anticipated material; this is one kind of metathesis. As before, we print the anticipated sound in boldface in both positions, but we enclose it in parentheses in the second position to indicate that it is not actually spoken there.

disintre**g**(**r**)ation (Bawden, p. 111)
stand**s**(**t**)one (Bawden, p. 111)
iodrofo(**r**)m
hem**l**(**m**)et
pat**r**(**t**)y
the si**ng**(**n**)al corps
whi**ks**(**k**)ers
whi**ps**(**p**)er
wi**st**(**s**) (Bawden, p. 111)

The same process, apparently, has yielded many forms that have gained more or less currency; for example, *calvary* for *cavalry, flim* for *film,* Latin *ascia* beside Greek *axinē* and English *axe.* Anticipation of the aspiration (that is, of an element of a phoneme) occurs in a number of words in Ionic Greek, e.g., *achantos* for *acanthos, Phytios* for *Pythios, bathracos* for *batrachos.*

4. Latin *ob* is cognate with Sanskrit *api* and Greek *epi;* its final consonant must be due to partial assimilation at some time or other.

ANTICIPATION WITH SUBSTITUTION AND LOSS

130. 4. Rarely the three processes hitherto discussed are combined. The resulting distortion is so great that the word or sentence is scarcely recognizable. It seems safe to say that a lapse of this kind never has any permanent effect upon a language.

The only examples of which I know are a few reported by Bawden (p. 106) and Meringer (pp. 22–37). Here again the anticipated material is printed in boldface and parentheses indicate material intended but not actually spoken.

put my (cup) **coat** in your **(coat)** pocket
accust(om)**im** (**him**)
viell(eich)**aucht (auch)**
hat s(i)**o**ch (d**o**ch), i.e., 'hat soch' for 'hat sich doch'

ANTICIPATORY LOSS (HAPLOLOGY)

130. 5. A peculiarly drastic kind of anticipation involves the loss of one of two identical phonemes or groups of phonemes and all that should stand between them. This phenomenon is often called haplology. In the following examples we set in boldface the recurring phonemes and enclose in parentheses all that is not actually spoken.

the at(**l**as of Ita)**l**y (i.e., *the atly*)
the ba(**tt**le of Wa)**t**erloo
Rh(**ine** w)**ine**s of that type
para(**lle**)**le**d (i.e., *parald*)

Repeated groups of phonemes may stand in immediate contact, so that there is no intermediate material to be lost.

n(**avy**) **avi**ator
P(**ost t**)**oast**ies

Haplology has received considerable attention because many forms like the above have become current in various languages. Very many examples might be cited, but a few will suffice.

English: lib(**ra**)**ry**
pro(**ba**)**bl**y
Glou(**ce**)**ster**
m(**ad**)**am**
humb(**le**)**ly**

Latin: scrīp(si)stī
amatu(s e)st
sē(mi)modius
Greek: hē(mi)medimnon

LAG ALONE

131. 1. Far less frequent than anticipation is the converse process of **lag,**[5] by which a phoneme or group of phonemes appears later than the speaker intends. The instances of lag fall into the same classes as those of anticipation, although for some of the categories I can cite very few. For lag alone, I have record of only two examples.

optic **t**up (for *cup*—Bawden, p. 103)
bush**es** and tree**ses**

The second example was reported to me as a poor jest; but I knew the man who said it, in a classroom lecture.[6] I am confident that the phrase was a genuine lapse, that he smiled when he realized what he had said, and that he disdained to correct himself.

LAG WITH SUBSTITUTION

131. 2. This is more common than any other kind of lag, just as anticipation with substitution is more common than any other kind of anticipation.

what **d**oes that (s)**d**ignify?
we have a m**ixed** group, they have a p(icked)**ixed** group
I want some men's **sh**ort-sleeved sports **sh**irts, made of (s)**sh**eer-(s)**sh**ucker
speed**y** and urg(ent)**y**
cath**o**de r(ay)**o**s
ling**ua** Franc(a)**ua**
so he will (say) **so** (Bawden, p. 103)
tidal w(a)**i**ve (Bawden, p. 103)
durch den **W**ald führt ein schöner (We) **W**ag

Several ancient Greek dialects show the effect of this process in counting (compare English *four five* instead of **whour five*—§ 130. 2. 1). The

5. Meringer's word is Postpositionen; his examples are grouped on pp. 59–69.
6. The late Charles Knapp of Columbia University.

general Greek word for 'seven' is *hepta,* and the initial consonant spread to the words for 'eight' and 'nine,' yielding *hoctō* and *hennea.*[7]

Contact assimilation of this sort appears in Latin *pellō* 'drive' from **pelnō, sallō* from **saldō* (cf. English *salt*), Old English *grētte* 'greeted' from **grēt-de* and *īecte* 'increased' from **īec-de*. Oscan and Umbrian regularly show *nn* where Latin has *nd,* as in the gerundive (*úpsannam* = *operandam*).

LAG WITH LOSS

131. 3. Lag with loss, like anticipation with loss, results in metathesis, and there is no possibility of distinguishing the two if the phonemes or groups stand in contact; *hemlet* for *helmet* may be analyzed as heml(m)et or as he(l)mlet. Since anticipation is far commoner than lag, it is the more probable explanation in all ambiguous cases. There remains only one example of which I am certain, *by help sending* for *by helping send*. Latin *cocodrillus* for *crocodillus* is a misspelling[8] that may represent a lapse of this sort (cf. Spanish *cocodrilo*).

LAG WITH SUBSTITUTION AND LOSS

131. 4. Lag with substitution and loss is even less common than anticipation with substitution and loss (§ **130. 4**). I have record of only one example: *I alwave said* for *I've always said*.

DISTANCE METATHESIS

132. Distance metathesis may be described as a combination of anticipation and lag, both with substitution and loss; it yields a third kind of metathesis. Here two phonemes or groups, separated by more or less intervening material, exchange places.

regular becomes *regural* (Bawden, p. 111)
elevate becomes *evelate* (Bawden, p. 111)
spilled becomes *slipt*
protoplasm becomes *plotoprasm* (Bawden, p. 110)
relevant becomes *revelant* (Bawden, p. 111)
rejuvenate becomes *rejunevate*

7. For details see C. D. Buck, Greek Dialects, p. 50.
8. See Sommer, Handbuch der lateinischen Laut- und Formenlehre, p. 214.

Putnam becomes *Putman*
can't draw checks separately becomes *secks cheparately.*
Gut und Blut becomes *But und Glut*
Freimaurer becomes *Fraumeirer.*
I feel so foolish becomes *I fool so feelish* (Bawden, p. 118)

The last four examples are typical Spoonerisms (§ 56). These are so grotesque that they are sure to be noticed, and no one would imitate them except in jest. Consequently they can scarcely have any influence upon the development of a language; as far as I know, none of them have turned up in the study of linguistic history.

MORE COMPLICATED METATHESES

133. The lapse, *has his hoat and cat* for *coat and hat,* involves the change of the series *h . . . h . . . c . . . h* to *h . . . h . . . h . . . c.*

The lapse, *presumably prular* for *plural,* involves the alteration of *r . . . l . . . l . . . r . . . l* to *r . . . l . . . r . . . l . . . r.*

DISSIMILATION [9]

134. In sharp contrast to the assimilative changes stand those in which a succession of identical articulations or phonemes or groups of phonemes is altered by the total or partial loss of one of them. In the following examples the recurring elements are printed in boldface and omitted material is enclosed in parentheses. We can distinguish three cases, the third of which, superficially at least, involves change rather than loss.

134. 1. A recurring phoneme or group of phonemes is lost as a whole. The omitted material is enclosed in parentheses. It will be noted that the recurring phoneme may be omitted in either its first or its second occurrence.

that sounds rather s(**t**)ilted . . . stilted
Gab(**r**)iel Ugron
oder ha(**s**)t Du's gesagt
ich bin b(**l**)oss . . . bloss verpflichtet
Sch(**r**)ei . . . Schreibebrief
still ob(**l**)iged (Bawden, p. 91)

9. Meringer's examples on pp. 91–98.

heights of (**h**)ate (Bawden, p. 96)
rep(**r**)ess (Bawden, p. 98)
the fifth line is le(**f**)t out
Univers**i**ty of (**Vir**)gin . . . of **Vir**ginia
histological s(**l**)ide
die (**D**)resdner . . . die **D**resdner

The history of various languages shows numerous results of this process. A few examples will suffice.

Latin latrō(**ni**)ci**ni**um 'robbery'
Latin p**r**aest(**r**)igiae 'jugglery'
Latin *flēbilis* 'lamentable' > French *faible* 'weak'
Latin *crībrum* > Spanish *cribo* 'sieve'
Proto-West-Germanic *breura-* > Old High German *bior,* Old English *béor* 'beer'

134.2. A recurring phoneme or group loses one of its elements.

You have to **s**(**t**)and **st**raight
It is in every sense a suffi**k**(**s**) e**x**cept . . .
der gan**z**e Insta**nt**(**s**)e**nz**ug . . .

Just so Latin *proprius* becomes Italian *propio,* and *quinque* becomes Vulgar Latin *cinque*. The dissimilation of aspirates in Sanskrit and Greek (cf. § **112**) gives us the reduplicated presents Sanskrit *dadhāmi* and Greek *tithēmi* 'I place' from prehistoric *dha-dhāmi* and *thi-thēmi* respectively. We usually consider Sanskrit *dh* and Greek *th* as unitary phonemes, but some scholars may prefer to consider them groups; our classification remains the same.[10]

134.3. A recurring phoneme is changed into a more or less similar phoneme in one of its occurrences.

The recurring phoneme is some kind of *r*.

de**r** Kerl war ganz verdattelt . . . verdatte**r**t
ein g**r**osser Gleu . . . G**r**euel
and the **r**ate lai . . . **r**aised
corn flitters (for f**r**itters)

10. Scholars who prefer to consider Greek *th* a group of two phonemes may appeal to the dissimilation of prehistoric *thrichos* 'of a hair' to *trichos* (beside nominative *thrix* hair'), where the *h* in *ch* has caused the loss of *h* in initial *th.* But the argument is not cogent; dissimilation is a matter of phonetics rather than of phonemics. In other words, whether we call Sanskrit *dh* and Greek *th* phonemes or groups of phonemes is only a question of terminology.

Similar instances have often been observed in the history of various languages. Latin *peregrīnus* becomes Vulgar Latin *pelegrīnus* (French *pèlerin,* Italian *pellegrino*); French *corridor* yields the Russian loanword *kolidor;* Greek *aristerā* 'left hand' becomes *alistera.*

The recurring phoneme is *l.*

übergebri . . . gebliebenes Fleisch

das ist doch ungrau . . . unglaublich

Such dissimilations are familiar to all readers of historical grammars and etymological dictionaries. I cite only the variant of the Latin suffix *ālis* (in *Ceriālis, annālis, aequālis,* etc.), which regularly appears as *-āris* after bases containing *l* (*angulāris, familiāris, intercalāris, ioculāris, mīlitāris, populāris*).

The recurring phoneme is *š.*

gibt's mir son . . . **sch**on einen Stich

die Zumbu**sch**ise (for Zumbu**sch**i**sch**e)

The recurring phoneme is *k.* Bernard Bloch is my authority for one such lapse.

Come into your **c**aramel-**c**olored **p**itchen (for **k**itchen)

135. Meringer (pp. 91, 93 f.) comments upon the extraordinary rarity of dissimilative lapses. I have listed here all English lapses of this sort that I have been able to discover. Under these circumstances the comparative frequency of just these dissimilations in our historical grammars is something of a mystery. For this reason I am inclined to accept, with some modification, a suggestion put forward some years ago by Albert J. Carnoy.[11] Probably the first impulse in all cases of dissimilation is toward the loss of one of the interfering articulations, phonemes, or groups of phonemes. Carnoy suggests that when Latin *peregrīnus* became *pelegrīnus* the loss of the trill in the first *r* may immediately (or presently?) have led to the substitution of *l* for the quite unfamiliar sound.

11. Transactions of the American Philological Association, 49. 101–113 (1918).

CHAPTER X

ANALOGIC CREATION

136. We have seen above (§ 103. 2) that the regularity of the phonetic laws is often obscured by apparent exceptions, which we have tentatively labeled "analogical" and reserved for treatment here. It is only in the position between vowels that *s* regularly becomes *r* in Latin; [1] final *s* after a vowel regularly remains in Latin, as *servus, genus, cīvitās, urbis, urbēs, amās, amāmus, amātis,* and innumerable other words. The final *r* in *melior, arbor,* and other nominatives, masculine or feminine, from stems which originally ended in *s* must be due to the change of *s* to *r* in other cases; after the old alternation of nominative *meliōs* : genitive *meliōsis* and *arbos* : *arbosis* had given way to *meliōs* : *meliōris* and *arbos* : *arboris,* the *r* was somehow carried into the nominative. That this is not the whole story, however, is shown by the persistence of several common types like *cīvitās* : *cīvitātis, dēns* : *dentis, amāns* : *amantis,* and *genus* : *generis;* why do we never find nominatives **cīvitat,* **dent,* **amant,* and **genur* or **gener?*

It has long been recognized that the spread of *r* from the other cases to the nominative of *melior* and *arbor* was induced by the numerous inherited *r*-stems such as *ōrātor* : *ōrātōris* and *soror* : *sorōris*. The logic of the process may be expressed by a formula of proportion; *ōrātōris* : *ōrātor* = *sorōris* : *soror* = *meliōris* : *x,* where the value of *x* is *melior*. The reason why *cīvitās* did not become *cīvitat* to match *cīvitātis* was the lack of model pairs; *caput* : *capitis* could not readily serve on account of the difference in gender. Similarly the neuter *melius* did not fall under the influence of the masculine and feminine *r*-stems, or even of the masc.-fem. *melior*. The neuter noun *genus* : *generis* was not affected by *ōrātor* or *soror,* but the compound adjective *dēgener* 'degenerate' (originally *dēgenēs;* cf. Greek *eugenēs* 'well born') follows the pattern of the masculine and feminine *s*-stems and *r*-stems.

1. In discussing the change of intervocalic *s* to *r* in Latin (§ 103) we promised an account of such analogical forms as *melior* and *arbor.*

Hermann Paul [2] confined the name analogy to the process that we have been describing. Some scholars have used the name also for other processes by which variations in form are made to conform more closely with variations in meaning, notably contamination, which we shall treat in the next chapter. These scholars have sometimes used the phrase *proportional analogy* for the process here under consideration; we shall follow Oertel [3] in calling it **analogic creation.**

137. The process of analogic creation has been observed in actual operation in several lapses.[4] One of my sons when a child suffered frequently from an ailment of the ear for which the standard treatment was irrigation with warm water. He reported the experience in the words, "I've been irrigated." Once he had some trouble with his nose, and warm water was poured into him by way of the nose. He reported, "I've been nosigated." Evidently the child interpreted the word *irrigated* as containing the word *ear,* and then created a new word on the proportion:

ear : irrigated = nose : x

Two children often dawdled over breakfast, and their elders tried to start a race by some such conversation as the following:

A. "I wonder whether Ann or Bradford will beat today."

B. "I think Ann will eat all her breakfast first."

A. "No, Bradford ate his orange first; he will surely beat today."

One morning Ann announced, "I bate Bradford; I ate all my oatmeal first." Although I can give no precise report of the conversation on this particular day, there is no doubt that the words *eat, ate,* and *beat* were scattered all through it, and the little girl herself used the form *ate* in the same sentence with the new form *bate.* Furthermore the only possible model in the English language for the pair *beat : bate* is *eat : ate.* We are fully justified in assuming the proportion:

eat : ate = beat : x.

A woman in New York said "Behave!" to her three-year-old son. In a few minutes he said, "Am I being haive now?" Some years later in Madison, Wis., a man said of his young son, "John has to behave," and

2. Prinzipien der Sprachgeschichte, 3d ed. pp. 96–109 (1898) = 5th ed., pp. 106–120 (1920).

3. Hanns Oertel, Lectures on the Study of Language, p. 163 (1901).

4. Some of these have previously been reported in Journal of the American Oriental Society, 57. 141 f. (1937) and references.

his three-year-old daughter immediately boasted, "I'm being haive." Long before either of these incidents a woman in Mobile, Ala., told her daughter to "behave," and was met by the claim, "I'm being haive." In view of the frequent injunction, "Now, be good!" we may safely set up the proportion:

be good : I'm being good = behave : x.

A man pointed out to his little son four airplanes flying over them, and remarked, "That is a formation." Presently the boy saw two more planes, and said, "There is a twomation." I do not know whether the child and his father use the same phoneme in *four* and *formation* (cf. § 25), but in any case the analogical proportion must run:

four : formation = two : x

A country parson is said to have met three boys of his parish and said to one of them, "What is your name, my lad?" "Sam," said the boy, and the parson corrected him, "Ah, Samuel." Then he asked the same question of the second boy, and corrected his answer, "Lem," with "Ah, Lemuel." The third boy wasn't going to be caught that way, and answered promptly, "Jimuel." If the incident is real, Jim's logic can be stated thus:

Sam : Samuel = Lem : Lemuel = Jim : x.

138. Bloomfield (p. 406) records the fact that psychologists sometimes object to such formulas as these "on the ground that the speaker is not capable of the reasoning which the proportional pattern implies. . . . We have to remember at all times that the speaker, short of a highly specialized training, is incapable of describing his speech-habits. Our proportional formula of analogy and analogic change, like all other statements in linguistics, describes the action of the speaker and does not imply that the speaker himself could give a similar description." In other words, we do not need to credit the speaker with the ability to state the problem but only with the ability to solve it when certain features in the situation have set the problem.

There is, however, available a more fundamental answer to the psychologists quoted by Bloomfield; young children sometimes justify their employment of an unusual form by citing the formula upon which it is based. Jespersen [5] tells of a Danish child, who was corrected for using a strong preterit *nak* 'nodded' instead of the usual

5. Language, its Nature, Development, and Origin, p. 131 (1922).

weak preterit *nikkede,* and who immediately retorted *stikker stak, nikker nak*. Bernard Bloch assures me that his three-year-old son has frequently defended himself by similar formulas, e.g., *sing sang, swing swang,* when corrected for saying *swang*. Of course children do not use a colon or a sign of equality or an *x* in stating analogic proportions, but they do sometimes state everything essential.

139. Such problems are extremely simple, and frequently a situation points up three terms of a proportion so clearly that no person can fail to infer the missing fourth term. Indeed, experiments performed for a different purpose upon young chicks and certain other animals indicate that these animals can solve very similar problems. Wolfgang Köhler [6] writes:

> A chick, trained with two grays, I and II (II being darker than I), always to choose II, will, after a while, when II and the new (darker) gray are given, in the majority of trials, not choose II but the unknown nuance III. The same experiments were performed on apes with size, and also with different hues of color. Several investigators have been able to confirm these experiments. We may conclude that animals react to such pairs as to wholes, either side of which has a definite character depending upon its "position" in the whole.

Here we have a number of ratios arranged in pairs as in our formulas for analogical proportion, except that the middle terms happen to be identical; thus

I : II = II : III.

140. In each of the analogic lapses so far discussed we can say with some confidence that the new form was created on the basis of one particular proportion, and probably, if we had complete information, a large part of all analogic creations would turn out to be of that type. As a matter of fact we rarely have enough information about an analogic lapse, and scarcely ever about an analogic creation that has been adopted by a language, to assign its origin to a single proportion.

A woman said to her husband at the breakfast table, "Daddy, please pass the cheese," whereupon her three-year-old daughter said, "Mummy, I want a chee too." The model may have been some pair like *trees : tree, bees : bee, pease : pea, crackers : cracker;* but the breakfast situation does not help us to fix upon any one.[7]

6. Gestalt Psychology, pp. 216 f. (1929).

7. Just possibly one of these or a similar pair (say *herrings : herring*) had recently occurred in the family conversation, but, if so, there is no record of it.

A woman, in describing a troublesome sore, said, "The bad—the baddest part of the sore." Evidently she was dissatisfied with the phrase as originally formulated (*the bad part of the sore*), since it was all bad, and the already spoken form *bad* inhibited the usual superlative *worst;* but there is no reason to suppose that any particular regular superlative furnished the model. Conceivably, since the sore was fevered, the pair *hot : hottest* came near enough to being used instead so that it has left its trace in *baddest;* [8] but there is no record that anything of the sort occurred.

I hear a personal name for the first time or I read one in a list; if thereupon I have occasion to speak of the man's house, I will at once say *Dumark's house* or *Etzel's* or *Gizzi's* or *Heman's* or *Lietor's* or *Nyquist's* or *Ramos's,* merely following the pattern of English possessive forms. The proof that particular models are not operative here is that I infallibly employ the ending [iz] after sibilants, [s] after other voiceless consonants, and [z] after other voiced consonants and after vowels. Even if I have just spoken a number of possessives with [s], *Lietor's* will inevitably be spoken with [z].

141. In case a language has a regular morphologic pattern, such as that of the English comparative and superlative, or the possessive case, or agent nouns in *-er,* the pattern itself rather than a particular pair of forms may induce new formations. Thus Latin nominatives singular in *-a* imply accusatives in *-am;* the first Roman to use the Greek place-name *Massilia* in a Latin sentence requiring the accusative would automatically have used the form *Massiliam*. He may of course have recently spoken or heard the forms *mēnsa* and *mēnsam* or *Rōma* and *Rōmam,* and in that case such a formula as

Rōma : Rōmam = Massilia : x

may tell nearly the whole story; it may rather closely parallel our formula (§ 137)

eat : ate = beat : x,

where no other model exists. But no Roman had to wait for a model to occur before he could say *Massiliam videō* or the like. The familiar pattern did not need to be reinforced by a concrete instance.

Of course the fact that Greek *Massiliā* was an *ā*-stem need have nothing to do with the process. The ablative *Massiliā* was furnished by the

8. Cf. the treatment of contamination in § 167.

Latin pattern although Greek had no ablative, and in popular Latin the Greek neuter noun *dogma dagmatos* 'doctrine' appears as *dogma,* accusative *dogmam.*

142. It is uncertain how free from competing patterns a morphologic pattern must be in order to operate without the help of a particular pair of words. Paul [9] ascribed the early Latin genitives in *-ī* from nouns of the fourth declension to the proportion

animus : animī = senātus : x,

where *animus* and *animī* symbolize all masculines of the second declension and *senātus* all masculines of the fourth that show *-ī* in the genitive. Eduard Hermann [10] suggested that a better statement would be

populus : populī = senātus : x,

since *populus* and *senātus* are members of a common phrase (*senātus populusque*). It is indeed probable that this very proportion did more than once induce a genitive *senātī;* but other standing phrases (e.g., *senātus lēgitimus, lacus Albānus*) may have suggested equally effective proportions, and undoubtedly there were occasional lapses with *senātī* or *adventī* that were due not to standing phrases but to casual collocations of words as unusual and unpredictable as the collocation of *eat* and *beat* that led to the new preterit *bate* (see above § 137). Besides, the pattern of the second declension, which Paul invokes in his ratio *animus : animī,* is much more common than that of the fourth declension (*senātus : senātūs*); it may have operated when no particular second declension noun was in the context.

143. That the frequency of a pattern is a factor in its extension by analogic creation is shown by the spread of the English negative prefix *un-* at the expense of the equivalent prefix *in-,* which we have in many loan-words from French and Latin. Since *un-* is prefixed to adjectives and participles much more freely than to nouns, we find it substituted for *in-* more frequently in the former context than in the latter; *unable* but *inability, uncivil* but *incivility, undigested* but *indigestion, unequal* but *inequality, unjust* but *injustice* are the usual forms.

144. When the result of analogic creation is a form hitherto unfamiliar to the community, there is no doubt what has happened; but the same process may produce a previously established form as well as

9. Prinzipien, 3d ed., p. 106 = 5th ed., p. 117.
10. Lautgesetz und Analogie, pp. 76 f. (1931).

another. When a little neighbor boy told me that I lived "in the two'th house" on our street, some such formula as *four : fourth = two : x* must have been at work; but if he had said *sixth* he might have been solving the problem *four : fourth = six : x,* or he might have been reproducing the word *sixth* from memory. When an adult speaks of the *three-hundred-sixty-seventh house,* there is a good chance that he has never heard that particular phrase, and that he is creating it anew. It is safe to say that a large proportion of any complicated morphology is used in this way. The classical Greek verb had over 600 different forms; if it had been necessary to remember each of these separately for each verb, it would have been difficult to master a large vocabulary. No doubt the Greeks frequently produced a verb form by analogic creation instead of by memory; they may have used relatively few model verbs more or less in the manner of our paradigms.[11]

145. If the process of analogic creation is a matter of logic, then our habit of saying that a derivative is formed by adding a suffix is inexact. Probably no one will maintain that we have at our disposal a stock of suffixes from which we select one as need arises. At any rate such a theory would break down completely for that part of the material where the derivative contains no additional element.

We have observed the pattern *eat : ate* giving rise to a new form *bate* to match *beat.* Similarly the pair *hide : hid* may induce *ride : rid.* Such internal variation is fairly common in the Germanic languages and it is characteristic of Semitic.

146. Still more difficult to describe by the terminology of affixation are the so-called inverse derivatives.

New Haven newsboys cry, "New York Times; buy a Time, Mister?" This may result from the other cry "New York Tribunes; buy a Tribune?" or it may reflect the common pattern of pluralization (with misinterpretation of the plural form *Times*).

A clerk in an Indiana dry-goods store spread out some stockings; then pointed to one pair and said, "Now this is a nice hoe." Many dealers in men's clothes recommend their wares with, "This is a nice pant."

Some years ago a character on the New York stage said, "Are you fond of Kipling?" The reply was, "I might be; how do you kipple?"

11. It is quite certain that model sentences serve in this way, and it may be that they are the nearest approach to our paradigms that actual speech provides. See below §§ 153–155.

Just so we get English *pea* from the borrowed collective noun *pease,* and *Chinee* and *Portuguee* are dialectic singulars of *the Chinese* and *the Portuguese.*

Latin *pugnāre* 'fight' is derived from *pugnus* 'fist'; it contains the suffix *-ā-,* which characterizes a large class of denominative verbs. From this verb comes the noun *pugna* 'fight.'

cēnāre : cēna = pugnāre : x

Evidently *pugnāre* is not historically a derivative of *pugna* although *cēnāre* is a derivative of *cēna,* and *pease* is not historically a derivative of *pea* although *bees* is a derivative of *bee.* As far as descriptive grammar is concerned, however, *pea pease* and *bee bees* follow the same pattern; and so do Latin *pugna pugnāre* and *cēna cēnāre.* Descriptive grammar must proceed by the analysis of the given phonetic material quite regardless of the history that may be behind it. Even from the historical point of view a suffix or other affix may have started with a bit of phonetic material that was mechanically added to a word or stem, as we shall see in § 187. We are merely contending that the usual process of forming derivatives is that of analogic creation, whether it involves suffixes, prefixes, infixes, or the subtraction of material already belonging to the primitive.

147. Compounds of a type already familiar to the linguistic community are also formed by analogic creation. We shall discuss in § 185 some of the ways in which compounds may develop out of phrases; it is only the spreading of a preëxisting type that concerns us now. When illuminating gas was introduced the English language already had such compounds as *firelight, candlelight,* and *lamplight,* and some such formula as *candle : candlelight = gas : x* produced the new compound *gaslight.*

148. The ancient Indo-European languages contain many compounds whose prior member is the bare stem of a noun or adjective; e.g., Greek *hippo-damos* 'horse-taming,' *drepanē-phoros* 'scythe-carrying,' *enches-palos* 'spear-wielding,' Sanskrit *Indra-guptas* 'Indra-protected, protected by Indra,' Latin *fāti-fer* [12] 'death-bringing,' *armi-ger* [12] 'arm-bearing,' *tri-angulus* 'having three angles, triangular.' This type of word formation

12. In Latin compounds the stem-vowel *-o-* of the prior member usually appears as *-i-* on account of the regular change of most short vowels to *-i-* in a medial syllable before a single consonant; (cf. *facilis : difficilis, faciō : reficiō*).

cannot have originated in any kind of syntactic structure presented by the recorded documents; the historic languages do not employ the bare noun-stem in phrases, although they do in compounds. It follows that the inherited models for the stem-compounds originated in prehistoric times, when practice differed somehow from that of Sanskrit, Greek, and Latin. One would like to say that in those days noun stems could be used in ordinary sentences, and that the stem-compounds were merely stereotyped phrases (like English *candlelight*); but some scholars doubt whether this was the case, and no proof is possible.

Just which of the recorded stem-compounds were inherited we do not know,[13] but we may perhaps assume, on the basis of Sanskrit *açva-yuk* 'yoking horses,' that one of them was Proto-Indo-European *ekwo-yuks*[14] (possibly with a by-form *ekwo-yugos*) 'yoking horses.' On the model of this inherited word, speakers of Sanskrit sooner or later formed other compounds beginning with *açva-*, such as *açva-dās* 'giving horses,' *açva-pālas* and *açva-pās* 'groom.'

Just so in Greek inherited **hippo-zygos* 'yoking horses' may have given rise to *hippo-damos* 'taming horses' and to other compounds with initial *hippo-*, such as *hippo-comos* 'groom,' *hippo-crotos* 'with the noise of horses,' *hippo-trophos* 'feeding horses.'

ANALOGY IN SYNTAX

149. Analogic creation sometimes originates or propagates a syntactic innovation. The colloquial phrase *I better go* (with simplification of the consonant group *-db-* of *I'd better go*) is quite familiar. Once a neighbor boy said to me, "I better [bɛtə] go now, bettn't I?" The model sentence must have been, *I ought to* [ɔtə] *go now, oughtn't I?*

The English group genitive (*the king of England's crown, Smith and Brown's store*) must have originated in such proportions as

the king : the king's crown = the king of England : x.

Smith : Smith's store = Smith and Brown : x.

The North German phrase *eine zue Tür* must be due to some such formula as

die Tür ist offen : eine offene Tür = die Tür ist zu : x.

13. Cf. Karl Brugmann, Grundriss 2². 1. 53; Wackernagel, Altindische Grammatik, 2. 1. 24 f.

14. The final *s* is required not only by such forms as Greek *sy-zyx* and Latin *conjux* but also by Avestan nominatives like *druxs* acc. *drujəm* 'lie.'

150. It is impossible to construe such a Latin sentence as *iniussū meō abiit*[15] 'he went away without my command,' since there is no noun *iniussus* 'a non-existent command'; but there is a negative of the participle *iussus* 'commanded,' namely *iniussus* 'uncommanded,' and there is a noun *iussus* 'command.' Our sentence is the normal solution of the problem,

iussus abiit 'having been ordered he went away' : *iniussus abiit* 'not having been ordered he went away' = *iussū meō abiit* 'at my order he went away' : *x*.

151. The Latin sentence of fearing, in the first person, is a fusion of originally independent sentences; *vereor nē id videam* 'I'm afraid that I'll see it' comes from *vereor* 'I'm afraid' plus *nē id videam* 'may I not see it,' which amounts to 'I'm afraid; I hope I won't see it.' A similar analysis of the third person, *verētur nē id videat,* would mean something like 'he is afraid; may he not see it' or 'he is afraid; I hope he won't see it,' and this is far from the actual meaning of the Latin sentence. We must assume some such formula as this:

vereor id quod videō 'I fear what I see' : *verētur id quod videt* = *vereor nē id videam* : *x*.

152. An important syntactic function of analogic creation is to produce new sentences that conform to an established pattern. An attendant at a public library uses many sentences like these: *Have you read Silas Marner? Have you read Lorna Doone? Have you read the Child's History of England?* As new books are published and purchased by the library, she substitutes new titles in her standing inquiry. For many years a familiar English sentence was *I notified him by messenger.* Then people said *I notified him by mail—by telegraph—by telephone.* Not until recently could the sentence run *I notified him by radio.* A similar series is

The coach is due at four o'clock.
The steamship is due at four o'clock.
The train is due at four o'clock.
The airplane is due at four o'clock.

The same process occurs when an individual speaker meets a new situation no matter how familiar it may be to the community. If a child has learned to understand or to say such sentences as *Where is mama? Where is George? Where is Jane? Where is the doll? Where is the top?,*

15. Such phrases are common in Cicero and Livy.

he will presently be able to substitute other nouns as he learns them in various contexts; he will understand on the first occurrence *Where is the cup? Where is the shoe?* and the substitution of *here* for *where,* together with the necessary change of intonation, will be automatic in any such sentence once he has learned that word.

153. Such analogic substitutions must function in a very large part of our speaking. We have seen (§ 144) that some at least of our morphology is probably created afresh for each use rather than repeated from memory. We speak and hear vastly more different sentences than different words, and therefore we must lean more heavily upon analogy in syntax than in morphology.

Unquestionably we learn by imitation and reproduce from memory a considerable stock of simple sentences: *What time is it? I must hurry. Please hurry. Please pass the butter.* These minimal sentences permit an indefinite amount of substitution by analogic creation. *What time was it? You must hurry. He mustn't hurry. Please pass the sugar.*

In the second place such sentences have beside them similar longer sentences that are also learned by imitation, e.g., *Please pass me your book.* Here we may substitute *give, lend,* or *hand* for *pass; the boy* or *the boy on your right* for *me; your French book, your other book, your book with the pictures,* or *the book that I gave you yesterday* for *your book.* Of course these substituted words and phrases must also have been learned by imitation or produced by analogic creation.

There is no assignable limit to the complexity of sentence structure that may be built up in this way. *Please pass me your book* admits the analogic substitutions involved in *He loaned me his book.* In the latter sentence substitute for *he* the phrase *the man who frequently brings us to town;* for *loaned* substitute *recently offered to lend;* for *me* substitute *his elderly neighbor;* for *his* substitute *an interesting and well-written;* for *book* substitute *book about a certain religious sect;* from other model sentences we can get additional phrases *to show the neighbor the comforts provided by that sect.* Thus we obtain the moderately long sentence *The man who frequently brings us to town recently offered to lend his elderly neighbor an interesting and well-written book about a certain religious sect, to show the neighbor the comforts provided by that sect.*

154. Such a sentence as this is often spoken rapidly and without hesitation; there is no time for recalling the numerous model sentences that form its foundation. It seems to follow that we somehow carry with us a sort of syntactic frame that has resulted from such phrases as *a book about horses, a book about religion,* and another similar frame that is an abstraction from *a certain man, a certain house, a certain political party,* etc. It is not for a linguist to discuss the means or manner of storing up these highly abstract frames, but there seems to be no escaping the conclusion that they are somehow stored up in each speaker. It is also clear that men differ enormously in their facility of using stored up speech-models; some speak rapidly and in sentences that seem to themselves fairly satisfactory, while others find it necessary to revise nearly every sentence once or many times in the process of utterance. The study of these revisions of sentences (sometimes called *anacolutha*) may be expected to throw light upon the nature of speech.

155. There are, then, two ways in which sentences are produced; a considerable number of sentences and phrases are repeated from memory; most of these are short and simple, but some are relatively long, and even whole series of sentences may be reproduced from memory (actor's parts, the patter of a museum guide, poetry committed to memory). Other sentences are formed by analogic creation. As far as I know, these are the only ways in which men can speak.

CONFLICT BETWEEN PHONETIC LAW AND ANALOGIC CREATION

156. We have noted several times that analogic creation induces apparent exceptions to the phonetic laws. In fact the study of the two processes has developed together; the recognition of numerous instances of analogic creation has enabled scholars to establish the regularity of the phonetic laws, and the prevailing regularity of phonetic change has thrown into relief the results of analogic creation.

As a rule the changes that we summarize in phonetic laws cut across the morphologic categories of a language and thus tend to confuse the system. In Proto-Indo-European the accusative singular of masculine and feminine nouns was marked by a final *-m* appended to the stem; *eḳwom* beside nominative *eḳwos* 'horse,' *eḳwām* beside nominative *eḳwā* 'mare,' *owim* beside nominative *owis* 'sheep,' *podm̥* beside nominative *pōts/pōd* 'foot.' In Greek, however, the phonetic laws (especially the law *m̥* becomes *a*) have obscured the formal mark of the accusative category; we find in these words accusative singular *hippon, hippēn, oin,* but *poda.*

In Latin no speaker could fail to interpret *ūndecim* 'eleven' as containing *decem* 'ten,' particularly since the succeeding numerals also ended in *-decim,* and the prior members also suggested the words for 'one, two, three,' etc. The French series *dix, onze, treize,* however, contains no clear reminder of the decimal system.

No Roman could avoid systematizing *inimīcus* as the negative of *amīcus,* even though the initial vowel of the second member of the compound had already been lost to a phonetic law. It is meaning alone that opposes French *ennemi* to *ami.*

In general, phonetic laws, just because they are regular, tend to introduce meaningless phonetic differences and thus cause irregularities in morphology.

A striking feature of analogic creation, on the other hand, is its lack of regularity. Since prehistoric times the English strong conjugation (*sing sang sung*) has tended to give way to the weak conjugation (*love loved*) by repeated instances of analogic creation (*love* : *loved* = *climb* : *x,* as against earlier *climb clomb*). Nevertheless numerous strong verbs still survive (*cling clung*), and many weak conjugation forms of analogic origin are today less common than formerly (*shine shined* as against *shine shone*). On the other hand not a few weak conjugation verbs have gone over to one or another class of the strong conjugation (*ring rang rung* as against Old English *hringan hringde*). A recent change of this sort is *dove* beside inherited *dived.* There are also such inconsistent conjugations as *show showed shown* (or *showed*); *shear sheared shorn* (or *sheared*). Alongside of the analogic substitution of the weak conjugation for the strong there has been much simplification of the strong conjugation itself. In Old English the singular (first and third) often differed in vocalism from the rest of the preterit; Old English *sincan, sanc suncon, suncen* gives rise to the Modern forms *sink, sank* or *sunk, have sunk.* But the singular *sank* is often lost by such a proportion as *they fell* : *he fell* = *they sunk* : *x;* the plural *sunk* is lost by such a proportion as *he fell* : *they fell* = *he sank* : *x;* hence we now say either *he sank* or *he sunk* and *they sunk* or *they sank.* In the similar preterit *ran,* the old plural *run* scarcely survives in standard English, although *have run* is as familiar as ever. In all this other processes than analogic formation are involved, but the crisscross operation of analogic creation upon the English strong verbs shows clearly that no man can predict when and how this particular process will behave.[16]

157. The way in which analogic creation repairs the damage done by phonetic law is neatly illustrated by the Attic Greek aorists (formed with suffix *-sa*). Certain phonetic laws (*-ts-* > *-s-*, *-ss-* > *-s-*, *-s-* between vowels is lost) yielded the aorists in the second columns below, and then analogic creation supplied the forms of the third column.

Presents	Inherited Aorists	New Aorists
pempō	epempsa	
deicnymi	edeixa	
elpizō	ēlpisa	
telō	etelesa	
lyō	*elȳa	elȳsa
tīmō	*etīmeā	etīmēsa
poiō	*epoieā	epoiēsa

We may summarize the conflict between these two tendencies by two paradoxes.

Phonetic laws are regular but produce irregularities.
Analogic creation is irregular but produces regularity.

16. For further details of the history of the English strong conjugation, see T. R. Lounsbury, History of the English Language, pp. 307–355, New York (1901).

CHAPTER XI

PROCESSES SOMETIMES CONFUSED WITH ANALOGIC CREATION

1A. CONTAMINATION[1] OF WORDS

158. Imagine a picnic party in the woods on a stifling summer's day. Suddenly one of the party hears a rustling of the leaves overhead, and feels a slight coolness on his cheek. He cries, "I hear a breeze," or "I feel a breeze," or perhaps he undertakes to say both at once and actually says part of each. Such may have been the situation in which was spoken the recorded lapse *I heel a breeze* (Bawden).

Momentary hesitation between two possible linguistic responses to a given situation (set of stimuli) is extremely common, and not infrequently it leads to a mingling of the two. Instances are *hithertofore* (*hitherto* × *heretofore*), *ruvershoes* (*rubbers* × *overshoes* — Bawden), and *soda countain* (*counter* × *fountain*). We call this process contamination, and the resultant locution is said to be a contamination of the underlying words or phrases.

Oertel[2] reports that Bishop Potter, former Anglican bishop of the diocese of New York, once said *evoid,* which he immediately corrected to *both avoid and evade.*

I once heard a woman say to her dog, "Now don't make an *upcry*" (*uproar* × *outcry*).

A man came home with a scratch on his face. His wife exclaimed, "Oh, you have a *blump!*" Inquiry showed that she had noticed both *blood* and a *lump.*

A woman said in answer to a question, "I haven't the *sleatest* idea" (*slightest* × *least*).

Meringer reports *Mansch* (*Mann* × *Mensch*); *Mundsprache* (*Mundart* × *Volkssprache*); *Mundweise* (*Mundart* × *Redeweise*); *überstaunt*

1. See Meringer, Aus dem Leben der Sprache, pp. 72–83; Bawden, A Study of Lapses, pp. 21–23.

2. Lectures on the Study of Language, p. 167.

(*überrascht* × *erstaunt*); *aus den Gleinern* (*Gliedern* × *Gebeinen*); *hergebildet* (*hergestellt* × *ausgebildet*).

159. Contaminations, like other lapses, sometimes leave permanent traces upon a language. Under the name of **blends** or **blendings** these have been frequently discussed.[3]

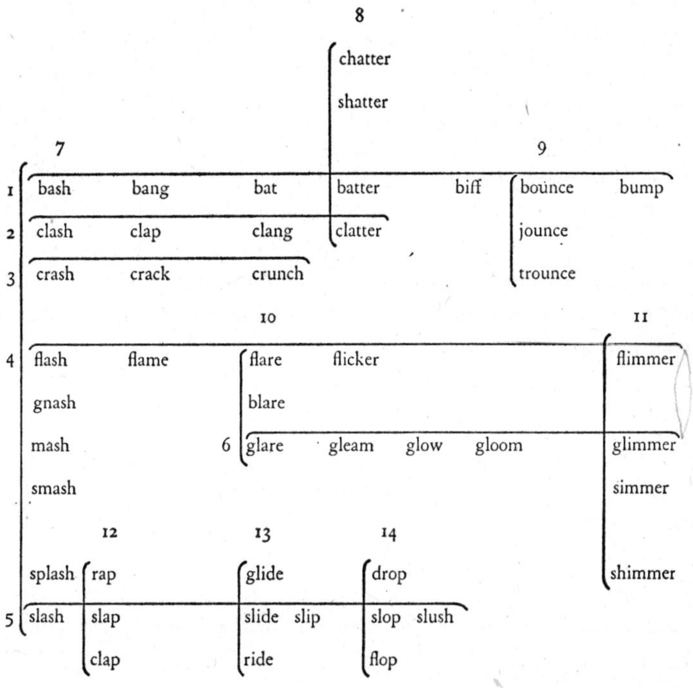

Figure 3

Some of the most plausible instances of contamination in conventional languages are to be found among the curious English words that are variously known as **symbolic words,** or **rime words.** A remarkable feature is their interlocking classification marked by identical initials or finals, as illustrated in Figure 3.

This is by no means a complete list of English rime words, or even of the words connected with those in the table; class 7 includes at least three other words, *dash, gash,* and *plash,* and *bump* belongs to another large

3. See Jespersen, Language, pp. 312 f.; Bloomfield, Language, pp. 244–246. A number of English rime words will presently be discussed in an article by Kemp Malone.

class including *clump, chump, dump,* etc. Figure 3 contains a selection of words, so arranged as to show their complicated interrelations. Some of the words in Figure 3 have cognates in other West Germanic languages, and are therefore inherited from Proto-West Germanic (*bounce, crack, gleam, ride*) and some are French loan-words (*bat, flame*). The beginnings of some of our classes were inherited (*gleam, glare; ride, glide*), and some other words in the table may be due to analogic creation; for instance, *flimmer* may come from the formula, *glare : glimmer = flare : x*. It is clear, however, that no set of unrelated etymologies can account for the extraordinary pattern presented by the table.

I can think of no plausible explanation aside from contamination. Of course it is impossible to reconstruct the actual history of the several words, but here are a few contaminations that would have been semantically and chronologically possible, as far as we know. The date of the earliest occurrence recorded in the Oxford Dictionary for each word is given in parentheses.

bat (1205) × mash (1000) > bash (1641)
clap (1375) × crash (1400) > clash (1500)
flame (1377) × glare (1400) > flare (1632)
gleam (1000) × shimmer (1100) > glimmer (1440)
flame (1377) × glimmer (1440) > flimmer (1880)
smack (1746) × mash (1000) > smash (1778)

The similarity of these suggestions to the lapses listed above is obvious; and no less obvious is it that just this sort of thing might give the interlocking classification of Figure 3.

1B. CONTAMINATION OF PHRASES

160. Contaminations of roughly equivalent phrases are: *Why did you do that for?* (*why . . .* × *what . . . for*). *No event is too extraordinary to be impossible* (Huxley—*too extraordinary to be possible* × *extraordinary enough to be impossible*). *No man is too big to decline the presidency* (Woodrow Wilson).

In trying to be agreeable to the cleaning woman one slushy morning, I said, "Lots of dirt tracked in these weathers" (*these days* × *this weather*).

The late Dr. Eva Fiesel reported German *sich protzen* 'boast' (*protzen* × *sich brüsten*). Meringer records *durch viele Jahre lang* (*durch viele Jahre* × *viele Jahre lang*); *jetzt ist mir rot* (*ist mir heiss* × *bin ich rot*); *wenn ich eine mutterlose Frau wäre* (*kinderlose Frau* × *nicht Mutter*).

A phrase originated in this way may be repeated by the original speaker or imitated by a hearer, and then substitutions may be made in it by analogic creation (**§ 152**). Such may be the origin of the curious use of *it* without an antecedent, as *The girl milked the cow and strained it* or *The First Church will employ an organist and a boy to blow it.*[4] Quite possibly the sentences *she milkèd the cow and strained the milk* and *she drew* (or *milked*) *the milk and strained it* were actually contaminated on the occasion recorded; but perhaps there were analogical models already in existence.

161. A fairly common type of sentence in colloquial Latin is illustrated by Terence, Heauton Timorumenos, 473: *Syrus cum illō vostrō cōnsusurrant* 'Syrus with that <slave> of yours *are* whispering together.' We have no right to ascribe this particular sentence to contamination rather than to analogic creation, but the type probably originated in contamination of two roughly equivalent sentences of unknown content but parallel with *Syrus cum illō vostrō susurrat* and *Syrus et ille voster cōnsusurrant.*

A similar statement may be made about the use, common in many languages, of a plural verb with a collective noun as subject. Shakespeare's *The army of the Queen mean to besiege us* represents a type that may have originated in confusion of *the army means* and *the soldiers mean,* or the like.

162. The puzzling Greek phrases *ho hēmisys tou chronou* 'half the time' instead of the anticipated neuter *to hēmisy,* and *ho pleistos tou biou* 'most of his life' for *to pleiston,* imply contamination of roughly equivalent phrases with adjective in agreement and substantival neuters followed by the genitive (*ho hēmisys chronos* × *to hēmisy tou chronou* or the like).

Just so Plautine *tē decōra* instead of *tibi decōra* 'things suitable for you' is undoubtedly due to contamination of ablative with *dignus* and dative with *decōrus,* but we cannot hope to learn when or in what

4. Such things in English are usually dismissed as mistakes, but when Cicero (Tusculanae Disputationes, 1. 2. 4) writes, *Ergō in Graeciā mūsicī flōruērunt, discēbantque id omnēs,* an editor comments: "*id,* i.e. music; its meaning is to be obtained from *mūsicī flōruērunt.*"

phrase or phrases the contamination occurred. The case is similar with Plautus' use of accusative after *ūtor* instead of the more usual ablative (cf. the roughly equivalent *adhibeō* with accusative).

163. Latin *quīn* from *quī-ne* often retains its etymological meaning 'why not?' but it is frequently used with an independent indicative or imperative in a rather vaguely strengthening sense. This second sense seems to have arisen in prehistoric times by the contamination of such sentences as *quīn dīcis* 'why don't you tell?' and *dīc* 'tell!' to form *quīn dīc*. Just how the emphatic *quīn* of the imperative sentence was transferred to non-interrogative indicative sentences we can only guess; perhaps we may set up such a formula as

dīc 'say!' : *quīn dīc* 'by all means say!' = *dīcō* 'I say' : *x*.

164. The shift of construction within a sentence, which classical scholars call **anacoluthon,** is a special case of contamination; it is usually found in rather long sentences, but these two short sentences have been cited as illustrations:

Plato, Apology, 210: *cai dialegomenos autōi, edoxe moi houtos ho anēr einai sophos,* 'and conversing with him—this man seemed to me to be wise.'

Terence, Hecyra, 286: *nōs omnēs, quibus est aliquis obiectus labōs, omne quod est intereā tempus lūcrōst,* 'all of us before whom trouble lies—the time between is gain.'

165. Instances are not lacking where one may suspect that an author has deliberately preferred a contamination to a more straightforward and normal phrase. In Aeneid, 6. 353, Vergil describes a storm-tossed ship as *spoliāta armīs, excussa magistrō* 'robbed of its tackle, shaken out of its helmsman.' Some of the editors note that we should expect rather *excussō magistrō* 'its helmsman shaken overboard' (metrically impossible as the line now stands), and that the expression has been influenced by the immediately preceding phrase. Perhaps we should rather assume influence from the ordinary prosaic word *prīvāta* 'deprived of'; but at any rate the sentence as we find it is strikingly similar to the contaminations cited above. And yet no reader would prefer (the metrically possible) *prīvāta* here, and no one would be tempted to make a closer parallelism between the tackle and the helmsman (e.g., *spoliāta armīs et magistrō*). If Vergil did not deliberately prefer the phrase preserved, harsh as it is, we must apparently suppose that this was one of the blemishes that he was going to eliminate in the intended revision of the poem. More or less of the same sort is Horace's rather frequent use of unmatched adjectives in such a way as to suggest the missing mate to each of them; e.g., Carmina, 3. 13. 6 f. (ode to the spring of Bandusia): *nam gelidōs īnficiet tibi rubrō sanguine rīvōs,* 'for he [the victim] shall stain your cool waters with his red blood.' The poet was tempted to say 'clear waters' and 'warm blood' and implies just that in addition to what he actually says.

2. FUSION OF INCONSISTENT ELEMENTS

166. So far we have been considering the contamination of two responses, both of which are appropriate under the circumstances. Most of the pairs we have cited have been roughly equivalent to each other; in some instances, however, the speaker's problem involved a choice between features of the situation. The picnicker (§ 158) was confronted with two scraps of evidence for the eagerly awaited breeze. The solicitous wife (§ 158) saw two evidences of a wound, dried blood and a swelling. The poet Horace avoided the choice between *gelidōs . . . calidō* and *limpidōs . . . rubrō.*

167. Very often parts of the speaker's situation are inconsistent with each other; he may, for example, have his attention called to events before his eyes while reporting past events or discussing a scientific problem; or the remark of a companion almost but not quite suppresses the remark he already had on the tip of his tongue. Meringer [5] discusses this matter at some length. Among his examples are these.

A classical scholar said, as he began to drink his beer, "Bei Prudentius habe ich *porgere* getrunken . . . gefunden."

Meringer had just found a long lost book of his own and he held it in his hand, but the conversation of the moment concerned a certain pocket handkerchief; he said, "Das Buch gehört gewiss ihnen."

Meringer held a cup in his hand, and said of an egg, "Wenn man es trinkt . . . isst."

I once heard a lecturer on linguistics repeatedly speak of *word* or *words,* and then translate a verb-form of a certain Indian language as 'he cut the word . . . the wood with a knife.'

Meringer reports *Beneinung* (*Bejahung* × *Verneinung*).

Personal names are often confused in this way.

5. Aus dem Leben der Sprache, pp. 39–54, see especially pp. 42–45.

The maid Fanny was in the room and Frau Meringer said to her husband, "Du Fanny . . ."

A student said to Meringer, "Der Professor Meringer . . . der Professor Schenkl liest auch am . . ." and then a date.

Meringer sat at table with his daughter Gretl and his wife Rida, and started to speak of a family friend named Lini: "Die Gre . . . die Ri . . . die Lini . . ."

It was a familiar experience in our household that our three children were addressed as *Gra-Ju-Cortland* or *Gra-Cor-Julian* or *Cor-Ju-Grace*.

168. If a word of a familiar phrase is spoken it sometimes carries the entire phrase with it even though the phrase has no bearing upon the actual situation. A woman said, "The Chicago fire . . . I mean the Chicago fair . . ." Another woman said of a surprising event, "I went into fits and starts over it." (The interfering phrase is *by fits and starts*). A speaker in a meeting of professors said, "when war is on the point of view . . . on the point of breaking out."

Common as such lapses are, it seems doubtful whether the fusion of responses to unrelated parts of a situation can have influence upon the development of a language; the chance of repetition is too slight.

3. CONTAMINATION vs. ANTICIPATION OR LAG

169. We have ascribed (**§ 130. 2. 1**) the initial phoneme of English *four* and German *vier* to a pre-Germanic anticipation of the initial of the next numeral (English *five,* German *fünf*); but this assimilation has sometimes been spoken of as an analogical change. While it is certainly not due to analogical creation, it is superficially similar to the change of *feel* to *heel* by contamination with *hear;* but it is not easy to imagine a recurring situation in which a speaker would hesitate between *four* and *five* and then choose one of them. In case of doubt he will normally say *four or five;* and just this phrase (or rather its pre-Germanic predecessor) no doubt reinforced the ordinary counting context in fostering the anticipation of *f*. It is clear that, when we have only the results of anticipation, it may be difficult to distinguish this process from contamination or even from analogic creation. The difficulty, however, is due solely to lack of complete records; there is scarcely any similarity at all between the three processes.

English *female* from French *femelle* might be expected to rime with *gazelle* or, after shift of the accent, with *hemal.* The actual vocalism of the second syllable evidently comes from the contrasting word *male.* But it is unlikely that speakers have frequently been confronted with a situation that caused them to hesitate between two responses containing respectively the words *male* and *female.* It is more probable that there has often been lag (cf. § **131. 2**) in the phrase *male and female.*

In many instances in which a word or phrase has clearly been influenced by another we can distinguish between contamination of rival responses and assimilation within a phrase only on the basis of inherent probability. On this basis we may suppose that Latin *rūsticānus* for *rūsticus* originated in some such phrase as *rūsticī et urbānī,* Christian Latin *merīdiōnālis* in a phrase like *merīdiānus aut septentriōnālis,* Greek *empodōn* 'in the way' from *em posi ē ec podōn* 'before the feet or away from the feet,' *opisthen* beside *opithen* 'behind' from *opithen cai prosthen.*

4. POPULAR ETYMOLOGY

170. Old English *scam-fæst* 'confirmed in shame (i.e., modesty),' hence 'modest' became early Modern English *shame-fast,* but this has now given way to *shame-faced,* which has taken the vocalism of *face* and enough of its meaning to suggest blushes. Similarly Old English *ūtmest, innemest,* and *norþmest,* all of which contained a superlative ending *-mest,* have been supplanted by Modern English *utmost* or *outmost, inmost,* and *northmost,* which show the form of the word *most.* Old English *brydguma* 'bridegroom' contained the word *guma* 'man,' but since this is now obsolete, we have given the compound a sort of meaning by substituting the word *groom.* French *carriole* 'a small, covered carriage' has, in English, become *carryall,* a name which inevitably suggests a function that the vehicle never had. Latin *liquiritia* yields English *liquorice* (which is only graphically assimilated to *liquor*), and this has become dialectic *lickerish.*[6]

These words all show a re-interpretation of linguistic material combined with a change of form which seems to result from the re-interpretation, but which might, on the other hand, be considered the

6. For parallel words, see Strong, Logeman, and Wheeler, Introduction to the Study of the History of Language, pp. 195–198 (1891).

cause of it. In *shame-faced* the present-day pronunciation is required if the final member is thought to be the same as that of *dog-faced,* but conversely, if we pronounce the word as we do we can scarcely avoid such an analysis, although the meaning which the analysis suggests is not quite satisfactory.

Scholars have long ascribed such words to **popular etymology,** a phrase which seems to contrast with scholarly etymology, scientific etymology, or the like. It seems to imply that the people discussed the etymology of such a word as *shame-fast* and decided that it was connected with *face.* There may well have been such discussion, since all men are more or less interested in the mutual relationship of parts of their words; but the discussion could scarcely begin until the pronunciation *shame-faced* was more or less familiar.

What we must assume is a situation that will give us the new form and the new analysis at once. We have observed a new and incorrect analysis of a word, but it involved no change of form. The child (§ 137) who said that he had been *nosigated* when they poured warm water into his nose had evidently found the word *ear* in the word *irrigate* that he had learned from the doctor. The child who called two airplanes a *twomation* had evidently assumed that the word *four* was an element of the unfamiliar word *formation* (§ 137).

In these instances we learn of the new analysis of the words *irrigate* and *formation* only from results elsewhere in the vocabulary.

That a new analysis may be synchronous with a misunderstanding of the sounds spoken scarcely needs proof; all of us frequently misunderstand what is said to us, while nevertheless we seem to get a complete although baffling meaning out of it. In my childhood I was surprised to learn that a certain boy was named *Blue Shepard;* I afterwards discovered that his name was *Hugh.* A student once told me that his German father conducted family prayers every morning and always closed with the petition, "Und das Kind, mag es unverletzet sein" (And the child, may it be unharmed). The child, not recognizing the solemn form *unverletzet,* understood "mag es unser letztes sein" (may it be our last).

171. The reason why a new analysis of a word is easily possible is that analysis of words and phrases is an essential part of understanding what we hear. Such a word as *unconditionally* owes its derivation from the noun *condition* to three processes of analogic creation more or less like these:

provision : *provisional* = *condition* : *conditional*
certain : *uncertain* = *conditional* : *unconditional*
uncertain : *uncertainly* = *unconditional* : *unconditionally* [7]

To put this in common terminology, the word *unconditionally* contains the suffix *-ly*, the prefix *un-*, and the suffix *-al-*. Just as the speaker or his predecessors put the word together, so the hearer may analyze it in the process of interpreting the sentence in which it occurs. He is reminded, more or less clearly, of the words *unconditional, conditional,* and *condition*. He may, in a suitable context, immediately ask, "Without what conditions?"

I do not mean to say that this kind of analysis normally determines the meaning of a word, but merely that such analysis is habitual with all hearers, and is therefore likely to mislead us at any moment. For the mature, native speaker, of course, most words are so familiar that the necessary correction is made at once; the most serious disaster that is usually possible is a pun. For instance, Henry M. Robinson [8] has a wife tease her husband for not asking her to dance, "You aren't as gallant as you were when a boy." He replies, "Well, you aren't as buoyant as you were when a gal." Here the husband hears the element *gal* in *gallant* and whimsically refuses to reject what he knows is a false analysis of the word.

A child, however, often lacks the linguistic experience that would enable him to make a correction. He is used to words and phrases beginning with *eye, mouth, ear,* etc., and for him it is not surprising that the remaining segment of such a word as *irrigate* or *formation* has no meaning at all; very likely he has heard of an *ear specialist* or of a *foursome* without experiencing any curiosity about the final member.

It would be more accurate perhaps to call this process and its result re-interpretation, but the term **popular etymology** has become so familiar that we may well retain it, if we remember that it applies to a naïve interpretation of speech, the sort of thing that becomes a pun when perpetrated by a speaker who knows full well that he is mishandling the language.

7. Cf. §§ 136–157. I have chosen model pairs at random; the argument is not affected by the choice. Furthermore the order of the three processes is of no importance.

8. Saturday Review of Literature, 27. 15. 13 (1944).

5. DELIBERATE CREATION OF WORDS

172. The changes that we have discussed in this chapter and the previous one occur automatically in the course of speaking and interpreting what is said to us. Very frequently men deliberately coin new words, and when they do so they do not ordinarily confine themselves to the procedures by which automatic changes occur. Even if they fully intend to follow models already set by the language, they are apt to go astray. The Reverend Professor William Whewell of the University of Cambridge, author of important works on the history of science, says, page 113 of the introduction to his Philosophy of the Inductive Sciences (1840):

> The terminations *ize, ism,* and *ist* are applied to words of all origins: thus we have to *pulverize,* to *colonize, witticism, heathenism, journalist, tobacconist.* Hence we may make such words when they are wanted. As we cannot use *physician* for a cultivator of *physics,* I have called him a *physicist.* We need very much a name to describe a cultivator of science in general. I should incline to call him a *scientist.*

Here we have a clear account of the origin of two familiar English words; *physicist* and *scientist* contain the suffix *-ist,* but they cannot have got it by the process of analogic creation that was described above (**§§ 136–157**). Whewell suggests the model *journalist,* but the formula

journal : journalist = physics : x = science : x

would yield *physicsist* or perhaps *physikist* and *scienceist.* Obviously Whewell corrected these results on the basis of other knowledge, which we may summarize as follows, although he pretty certainly would not have put it just so. In words borrowed from Latin through French [k] is changed to [s] before the suffixes *-ist* and *-ism* (*publicist* beside *public, cynicism* beside *cynic* and *cynical*). The combining form of *science* is *scient-,* as in *scientific.* These are things that the naïve speaker of English does not know, and that few speakers would have time to apply correctly while forming a sentence.[9]

173. Another word of whose origin we have some record is *gas,* about

9. Once while talking to a group of scholars I wanted to match the term *Germanist* with a derivative from *Romance;* I said *Romanticist*—and to this day blush at the memory. If I had had time to think I would have said *Romanist.*

which the Dutch chemist Van Helmont says,[10] "halitum illum *gas* vocavi non longe a *chao* veterum secretum." Here we seem to be told that *gas* is a loan-word (with change of meaning) from Greek *chaos;* but it can scarcely be just that in view of its form.

A scientific term more recently invented is *gene* 'that part of the chromosome which determines the inheritance of a particular character.' The term was chosen, after considerable discussion, for its brevity, its resemblance to such words as genetic, generate, etc., and its freedom from specific implications.

A very familiar class of newly created words consists of the names of biological genera and species. For historical reasons these are supposed to be in Latin, but almost anything with a Latin termination goes, and occasionally even this requirement is waived; examples are *Columbigallina passerina, Dolichoglossus kowalewskii, Laelia pumila dayana, Malanoplus femur-rubrum, Phycis chuss.* It makes little difference whether these labels conform to the morphological pattern of any language as long as they are usable by the specialists concerned. Our present point is that they are inevitably conscious inventions of one man or a small group.

174. Advertising names are formed in many different ways, but nearly always quite arbitrarily. *Socony* gasoline is named from the initial letters of the *Standard Oil Company of New York*. *Finast* is the trade name of merchandise handled by the *FIrst NAtional STores.* A new *Hydra-Matic* drive, it is claimed, "combines a fluid coupling with a fully automatic transmission." The name of a kind of refrigerator is *Frigidaire,* which appears to be a possessive compound like *redhead, flatfoot, Greatheart,* etc. Other compounds of the group, however, are all accented on the prior member, and we are puzzled by the spelling with silent final *e.* Possibly the spelling was chosen just because a useless final *-e* is thought to lend distinction (cf. *shoppe*), and this suggested the final accent that we have in many loan-words from the French (*millionaire, chiffonier*).[11]

Ever since Lewis Carroll in Through the Looking-Glass set the fash-

10. According to the Oxford English Dictionary s.v.

11. Like many loan-words from the French, *Frigidaire* is subject to the general English tendency to shift the accent to the initial syllable; but it is still most frequently accented on the final.

ion, the coining of ingenious new words has had a remarkable vogue among certain literary artists. Perhaps the magazine Time has been most fertile with its telescoped words like *cinemasculated,* its compounds in *-man* (*glider-man, New York Times-man*), its participial adjectives (*balding*), and other oddities.

Some artists' and advertisers' inventions get into linguistic literature from time to time; scholars attempt to work them into their treatment of analogic creation, contamination, or some other ordinary linguistic process. The truth is that *electrolier* was not "formed on the analogy of *chandelier*" in at all the same way as *cows* was formed on the analogy of some other plural or after the pattern set by many plurals; it is the product of some artist's (or advertiser's) careful reflection. We must eliminate such words, as far as possible, from the material upon which we base our treatment of analogic creation.

Coining words, like writing books, is a function of artists. Whatever science has a connection with either process is an applied science; these particular topics belong to rhetoric. In so far as linguistics is the study of the principles and processes that underlie the development and use of languages it is a pure science. We linguists need not attempt the hopeless task of classifying the inventions of advertisers, philosophers, and—linguists. We, like other scientists, must adopt and use a set of technical terms, but this is at bottom an artistic, not a scientific problem. No scholar has a right to demand, as one has, on scientific or linguistic grounds that we discard the familiar and convenient word *phonemic* for the reason that if an ancient Greek had coined an adjective from the noun *phōnēma* he would probably have produced *phōnēmaticos.*[12]

12. Cf. Joshua Whatmough, Classical Philology, 38. 211 (1943); George M. Bolling, *ib.,* 39. 104 (1944); Carl D. Buck, *ib.,* 40. 47 (1945).

CHAPTER XII

CHANGE OF VOCABULARY

175. Any man's available speech material is a complete record of his conscious experience as far as he remembers it. That is to say, he can, on occasion, give a report of any part of it. The words and phrases that he has at his disposal, if they could be collected, would serve as an index to his life, his reading, and what he has been told, except that every speaker has forgotten some of his experience and some of the words he has once known (e.g., many proper names). The size of a man's vocabulary, however, is extremely difficult to determine; the total would be very different for words understood, for words spoken, and for words written. Jespersen [1] discusses some estimates ranging from Max Müller's grotesque but widely quoted guess of 300 words for an English farm laborer's vocabulary to Professor Holden's estimate of his own at 33,456 words. The latter figure is doubtless nearer the truth than the former; but neither this nor any other estimate can have any objective value. For example, I understand the word *hemal* (cited above), but I have never used it and probably never shall.

In the same way the words and phrases of a linguistic community must form a sort of index of the experience of all the members of that community, including all that they know about the past and all that they imagine about the future. Consequently the history of a community must be reflected in changes of their vocabulary; as objects and ideas are forgotten the corresponding words or phrases must go out of use, and as new knowledge is gained linguistic forms to match it appear.

Thus our culture has little present need for the words *distaff, flail, alchemy,* and *fief;* flails, to be sure, are still in use in some remote regions, and several of these words are still familiar in figurative expressions: he *flailed* about with his arms; the subtle *alchemy* of her presence. All four words are still frequently used in discourse about the past. A word that seems to have vanished completely, except for use by

1. Growth and Structure of the English Language, pp. 211–214 (1905).

a few historians of armor, is *brachal* 'protective armor for the arms' (latest citation in the Oxford Dictionary, 1668). New words recently demanded by changes in culture are *locomotive, telegraph, radio, movie, protoplasm, endocrine, pleistocene, electron, ion, radar.*

TABOO

176. In every human community, as far as we know, certain acts must not be performed under certain circumstances, although compelling reasons for the inhibition are difficult to find, or the reasons given in the community are arbitrary and fanciful. Some such inhibitions are widespread among mankind. All men show modesty about voiding the excrements and about sexual intimacies in the presence of others; but the animals, even those most similar to man, show no such behavior and neither do young children. Furthermore there is the utmost variation in detail between different human communities and between the habits of the same community at different times. A large proportion of mankind are more or less shocked at nudity, but not certain "primitive" peoples, nor were the ancient Greeks, nor are some groups of our fellow citizens. Differences of opinion about who may marry whom are familiar; is it right for a man to marry his deceased wife's sister? Or his first cousin? Or a woman who has been divorced? Among us the marriage of brother and sister is strictly forbidden, but such marriages have been preferred in more than one royal family (e.g., the Incas of Peru, the Ptolemies).

The Polynesian word *taboo* has been borrowed as a designation of this irrational [2] avoidance of certain acts. Its use originally implied that the Polynesians and other "primitive" peoples are peculiarly subject to these queer inhibitions, but we ourselves live in glass houses. Taboo is found in much the same departments of human life the world over, namely, religion, sex, excretion, dress, eating, social status.

177. Taboo concerns linguistics because it applies to many words. To a certain extent the things that may not be touched and the acts that may not be done may not be mentioned either. Here belong the famous

2. The word *irrational* in this connection means that the reasons given, if any, differ from place to place and from time to time; it does not mean that the author is in favor of any of the practices whose avoidance he calls irrational. He does not, for example, advocate the marriage of brother and sister.

"four-letter" words of English; some of these are more strictly taboo than any others in the language; two of them are too indecent to be printed in the Oxford English Dictionary, and American dictionaries are generally still more prudish. An excellent scholar [3] has published a scientific article about one of them without ever mentioning the word at all. On the advice of friends I shall not here print either of the words that are omitted by the Oxford Dictionary. Only slightly less objectionable is the word *arse* and its variant *ass,* which is labeled by the Oxford Dictionary as a "vulgar and dialectic spelling and pronunciation of *arse.*" Although this is the prevalent form in America, it is not mentioned by the American supplement of the Oxford Dictionary,[4] or by the latest Webster. The taboo against this word is so strong that the animal with the homonymous name can scarcely be mentioned in some circumstances; teachers of young boys have to avoid the biblical story of Balaam's ass for fear of the boisterous reaction of their auditors.

178. An important feature of linguistic taboo is the emotional shock of violating it; to some speakers this gives a delightful thrill until familiarity makes the whole experience dull or even annoying. Hence small boys write several of the four-letter words on walls or sidewalks, while soldiers, teamsters, etc., make expletives out of them.

179. These words, however, have a perfectly definite meaning that frequently needs to be expressed. It is impossible to rear young children without substitutes for some of the four-letter words and so every family has a stock of nursery terms; they differ considerably from family to family, and they are handed down in the female line (with occasional loans from schoolgirl acquaintances). In polite society a common euphemism is *to wash one's hands.* For *privy,* probably once a euphemism itself, we say *water-closet, bathroom, toilet, rest-room,* etc.; the large variety because the substitutes for taboo words tend to become infected themselves.

180. Verbal taboo in English is usually far weaker than this, and subject to much wider variation from time to time and between parts of the linguistic community. The British avoidance of the word *bloody,* now less strict than formerly, was never shared by Americans, except those in close touch with England. The word *leg* was formerly taboo in

3. Allan Walker Read, An Obscenity Symbol = American Speech, 9. 264–278 (1934).
4. A Dictionary of American English on Historical Principles, Chicago (1938–44).

America and is still in some rural districts. Many years ago I saw this sign in a railroad station:

PLEASE DO NOT EXPECTORATE (spit) ON THE PLATFORM[5]

181. A series of articles in American Speech[6] provides evidence on the milder kinds of taboo among college students in Georgia and Tennessee. Stedman asked students to submit lists of "coarse and obscene words" that the student himself avoided. He got such words as *guts, stink,* and *belly,* the last being the most offensive word that these young people could bring themselves to write down and submit to a professor. Hunter and Gaines submitted a list of 62 words to their subjects and asked them to check those that they used freely or with varying degrees of reluctance (the list contained only the milder sort of taboo words). The eight least freely used words in the list are *bitch, puke, whore, bastard, belly, guts, belly-ache,* and *harlot.* Less objectionable are *vomit* (for which the students substitute *throw up, regurgitate,* or *unswallow*), *breast* (substitutes: *bosom, chest*), *pants, sweat.*

182. Stedman's second paper was based upon lists of words avoided as being affected or effeminate; many of them are substitutes for words subject to a mild sort of taboo. The most unpopular words submitted are *limb* 'leg,' *retire* 'go to bed,' *it is I, expectorate, elegant, cease, prevaricate, deceased, angry.* Here we see a reaction against taboo that can scarcely be distinguished from the stylistic choice between such synonyms as *kick out* and *expel; quit, stop,* and *cease; gang, crowd,* and *group; let* and *allow.* The word is chosen to suit the occasion, and one speaker's choice differs from another's.

SLANG

183. Such a situation inevitably leads to the introduction of new words and phrases. Some speakers need new substitutes for words which for them have become taboo under certain circumstances. And

5. For other taboo words of restricted currency, see H. L. Mencken, The American Language, 4th ed. pp. 300–318, New York (1936).

6. J. M. Stedman, Jr., A Study of Verbal Taboos, 10. 93–106 (1935), Affected and Effeminate Words, 13. 13–18 (1938); Edwin Hunter and Bernice Gaines, Verbal Taboo in a College Community, 13. 97–107 (1938).

other speakers search for new terms that have more flavor or raciness than any actually available. Hence the endless procession of **slang;** new words introduced by the wits of the community, quickly adopted by the young, and soon abandoned for something fresher. In the year 1917 I published [7] the following paragraph; note that all the examples cited seem more or less archaic thirty years later.

Many new words are due to a desire for novelty. Such are the slang words which spring suddenly into popularity and for a few months seem amusing enough to enliven the dullest conversation, but which presently send a shudder down the spine of one whose slang is up to date. Not long since [i.e., in 1901] I heard a professor of my acquaintance remark jauntily, "You're off your base." That phrase was once as fresh and spicy as *have a heart* or *do one's bit* is now; but to use such antiquated slang today is equivalent to labeling yourself a *has-been*. Who wants to call his partner in the Plattsburg military trot a *lulu* or the music *hot stuff?* Yet that is what one said in the days before the schottische went out of vogue! George Ade's Artie called dollars *cases* or *simoleons*. About the year 1910 [read: 1900] the word *skiddoo* was a favorite imperative for a contemptuous dismissal.

HOMONYMY

184. Many, perhaps most, languages show a very large tolerance of homonyms. English *reed* and *read* (present tense), *red* and *read* (past tense), *sew* and *sow, fur* and *fir, pen* (for writing) and *pen* (for cattle) rarely interfere with each other; the context almost inevitably shows which is meant. In a highly inflected language homonymy is even less likely to cause confusion; Latin *aggere* 'bring to,' and *aggere* 'by means of a rampart,' *annō* 'I swim to' and *annō* 'a year ago,' *facis* 'you make' and *facis* 'of a torch,' *faciēs* 'you will make' and *faciēs* 'face,' *ī* 'go' and *ī* 'they' can never have caused any real difficulty. It is only when each of a pair of homonyms can occupy the same position in the same sentence that misunderstanding is frequent. In that case the speakers are compelled to do something to help themselves. Here is an example.

In a part of the United States *-en* has become *-in,* so that *pen* and *pin* are homonyms. A seventh-grade pupil said to her teacher, "Miss ——, kin I have a pin?" The teacher searched in her desk and brought out a pin. "No'm," said the child, "I want a writin' pin." It happened that

7. Linguistic Change, pp. 107 f.

the teacher spoke a dialect which keeps *pen* and *pin* apart; perhaps otherwise the schoolroom context would have given her the necessary clue.

In other cases confusion must be very frequent, although I cannot recount instances. R. J. Menner [8] cites evidence that in parts of New England *stout* 'strong' and *stout* 'fat' are in conflict, and that the former is being crowded out. Similar rivalry exists between *mad* 'insane' and *mad* 'angry,' and between *clever* 'good-natured' and *clever* 'handy.'

The evidence cited by Menner indicates that the rivalry between *sad* 'satisfied' and *sad* 'sorrowful' has contributed to the loss of the former since 1450, although several intermediate meanings may have played their part.

English *silly* 'happy, blissful,' obsolete since 1482, must have conflicted with *silly* 'innocent,' *silly* 'helpless,' and *silly* 'insignificant,' and these, in turn, succumbed to *silly* 'foolish' by the middle of the seventeenth century.

The Old French homonymy between *moudre* 'milk' (from Latin *mulgēre*) and *moudre* 'grind' (from Latin *molere*) has led to the loss of the former word in Modern French. In Provençal the two words both survive as *molzer* and *molre* respectively. The proof that the homonymy is responsible for the loss in French is that the phonetic change that yielded Old French *moudre* 'milk' is confined to the same region as the loss of the word in dialects of the present day.[9]

In a similar way Gilliéron [10] explains the absence of the expected form of Latin *gallus* 'cock' in the southwest corner of France. In precisely this region Latin *cattus* 'cat' and *gallus* would both yield modern *gat*. Hence various makeshift terms have been substituted for *gat* 'cock.'

Old Provençal had two words *trau* 'beam' and *trauc* 'hole.' On the loss of final consonants they became homonymous, and today the local dialects have replaced one or the other word by a substitute.[11]

8. Language, 21. 59–76, especially 70–73 (1945). Of course it is irrelevant for our purpose whether homonyms are historically the same word (*stout*) or different words (pen, pin). Cf. R. J. Menner, Language, 12. 229–244 (1936); Edna R. Williams, The Conflict of Homonyms in English, New Haven (1944).

9. Albert Dauzat, La géographie linguistique, p. 65 (1922).

10. Gilliéron and Roques, Études de géographie linguistique, p. 50 (1912); Cf. Dauzat, La géographie linguistique, pp. 65–67; L. Bloomfield, Language, pp. 396–398 (1933).

11. Dauzat, La géographie linguistique, p. 68.

SOURCES OF NEW WORDS

Composition

185. When a culture acquires a new feature or when an old term comes to be avoided through taboo or homonymy or for any reason whatever, a new term is needed. Frequently the first recourse is to a phrase; recent inventions have been called *horseless carriage, moving picture, wireless telegraph, atomic bomb.* When the Greeks under Cyrus encountered the ostrich in the Arabian desert they named it *ho megas strouthos* 'the big sparrow.' In most cases such a name is soon eliminated in one way or another, if the new cultural feature is at all important (cf. § **202**). If it is kept it may in time lose some of the characteristics of ordinary phrases and become more like a single word. English *railroad* is unlike the phrase *rail fence* in having an accent on the first syllable. It also differs in having a meaning that cannot be inferred by the ordinary processes of analysis.

In most contexts a *rail fence* is called merely a *fence,* but a *railroad* is called a *road* only if the context clearly shows that the word is an abbreviation for *railroad* (e.g., *The C.I. and L. is one of the important roads of the state,* as against *the roads in this county are not very good*). In general a *railroad* is not called a *road* at all.

English *railroad* is a compound that has developed out of a phrase. So is Latin *dēnuō* 'anew' from *dē novō, vēneō* 'I am sold' from *vēnum eō* 'I go to sale, am offered for sale,' *animadvertō* 'I notice, punish' from *animum advertō* 'I turn (my) attention to.' New grammatical machinery frequently arises in this way, e.g., Latin *quāre* (from *quā rē* 'from what thing'), or *quamobrem* 'wherefore,' *quamquam* 'although,' *itaque* 'therefore,' English *nevertheless, although,* German *wenngleich.*

186. While types of compounds are often, perhaps usually, developed out of phrases, we have noticed that a type, once it has been set, may be extended indefinitely by analogic creation. Such are the vast majority of the compounds of Indo-European languages; English *flat-foot, red-head, finger-ring,* German *Befehls-haber* 'commander,' as well as Greek *brachy-bios* 'short-lived,' *an-ydros* 'waterless,' and Sanskrit *veda-vit* 'veda-knowing' and *jīva-putras* 'having living sons.'

Derivation

187. A second common source of new words is provided by **derivation.** We have seen that derivatives of all sorts are formed by means of analogic creation, but we still have to consider the origin of the models upon which the new forms are based.

Many suffixes are known to have developed out of the final members of compounds; thus English *friendly* is the modern form of Old English *freond-līc* (adjective) and *frēond-līce* (adverb), and in Old English the word is clearly a compound whose final member is *līc* 'body, form.' Equally clear are the suffixes of *friendship* (cf. *shape*), *fearful* (cf. *full*), *childhood* (Old English *hād* 'rank, social position'), *kingdom* (Old English *dōm,* whence English *doom,* 'statute, judgment, jurisdiction').

French *aimerai* 'I shall love' represents a late Latin phrase *amāre habeō.* French *lentement* 'slowly' comes from Latin *lentā mente;* note that the English suffix *ly* comes from a word meaning 'body' and the corresponding French suffix from a word meaning 'mind.'

We seem to have a similar development in Oscan *húrtín Kerríiín* 'in luco Cereali' 'in the grove of Ceres.' The locative ending *-ín* must have resulted from contraction of the inherited locative ending *-ei* with the postposition *-en* 'in,' upon loss of intervocalic *y* (*-ey-en* > *-ēn,* which regularly yields Oscan *ín*). Since intervocalic *y* was lost in Proto-Italic, and since *ē* of later origin was retained (as in *keenztur* 'censor'), it is necessary to assume the persistence of the conglomerate ending *-ēn* > *-ín* from Proto-Italic times to the date of the bronze tablet on which we find it. The use of the ending *-ín* in the adjective as well as in the noun combines with the history of the formation to prevent our analyzing it here as case ending plus postposition.[12] The simple locative in *-ei* also survives in Oscan and the paucity of our material prevents our establishing any local or syntactic distinction between them.

188. In several instances affixes have developed from accidental differences of form, which originally had no connection with variations of meaning. English *my* and *thy* are historically by-forms of *mine* and *thine* that were, in the early fourteenth century, used before words be-

12. See Buck, A Grammar of Oscan and Umbrian, p. 34 (§ 41a), p. 53 (§ 82. 1), p. 117 (§ 171. 7).

ginning with a consonant. Somewhat later the short forms came to be used consistently before all nouns, and the longer forms as predicate adjectives (*my house* but *the house is mine*). Then new forms *hisn, hern, ourn, yourn, thiern* were analogically created to match *mine* and *thine*. These new forms have now been banished from the standard language.[13]

English *ox,* plural *oxen,* comes from Old English *oxa,* whose stem ended in *n* in all cases except only the nominative singular. It was not until Middle English that *n* was excluded from all cases of the singular and *n* thus became a mark of the plural; thereupon it was analogically transferred to other words, e.g., *synnen* 'sins,' *treen* 'trees.'

In German, *-en* is still a common plural suffix, and so is *-er,* which is also an old stem final (cf. Latin *genus genera*).

189. There has been a long discussion as to whether the Indo-European inflections originated by agglutination or in some other way.[14]

The truth is that nearly all Indo-European inflectional endings and a large majority of the stem-forming suffixes are of unknown origin; most of them, in fact, existed in Proto-Indo-European, and may even then have lost all traces of their origin. Only one clear hint emerges from the discussion; we can demonstrate an agglutinative origin for more suffixes than an adaptive origin.

190. Very commonly two suffixes are combined and treated as one. From Latin *iūdex* 'judge' was derived a verb *iūdic-ā-re* 'to be a judge,' and from this an abstract noun (fourth declension) *iūdicā-tus* 'the position of being a judge, judgeship.' Then the formula

iūdex : iūdicātus = cōnsul : x

yielded the noun *cōnsulātus* 'consulship' although there is no verb *cōnsulāre* 'to be a consul.' Similarly beside *decemvir* 'member of a board of ten' we get a noun *decemvirātus*.

Latin adjectives in *-ius* and abstract nouns in *-ia* from agent nouns in *-tor* are very common, e.g., *nāvis mercātōria* 'a merchant ship,' *victōria* 'the state or position of victor,' but such words are also used in direct connection with the underlying verbs and in such a case the suffix is

13. For details see Lounsbury, History of the English Language, pp. 275–281 (1901).

14. See Hanns Oertel and Edward P. Morris, Harvard Studies in Classical Philology, 16. 63–122 (1905) and references.

rather *-tōrius*. When Gelasimus, in Plautus, Stichus, 227, offers for sale *ūnctiōnēs Graecās sūdātōriās* he means 'Greek rubdowns that will make you sweat.' In Livy, 2.50.2 we read, *gēnsque ūna populī Rōmānī saepe ex opulentissimā, ut tum rēs erant, Etruscā cīvitāte victōriam tulit* 'the one nation of the Roman people often gained the victory from the Etruscan state, richest of all, as things were then'; but there is no *victor* implied in the context; only the *gēns victrīx*.

Very often it is impossible to point to analogic formulae that would account for the extension of a suffix. Latin had a suffix *-nus* that was often appended to *-ā-stems* (*Rōmā-nus : Rōma*); from these a suffix *-ānus* was somehow abstracted [15] and it appears in such words as *urb-ānus, oppid-ānus* (*: oppidum*) *Octāvi-ānus* (*: Octāvius*). Since there was a word *octāvus* 'eighth,' and presumably in prehistoric times a praenomen **Octāvus,* it was once possible to analyze the name *Octāv-iānus,* and so to form new derivatives *Mīlōn-iānus, Cicerōn-iānus*. Latin as recorded scarcely contains workable models for the formation of the extended suffixes, *-ānus* and *-iānus*.

15. That such derivations belonged to Proto-Italic is shown by Oscan *Púmpaiians, Núvlanús* (nominative plural), etc. Perhaps *-ānos* also is pre-Latin.

CHAPTER XIII

CHANGE OF MEANING

SEMANTIC CHANGE ERRATIC

191. While the regular operation of the phonetic laws makes it possible to recognize a connection between widely different forms in related languages, there is no similar clue to help us trace the changes which have affected the meanings of words. No scholar can doubt the etymological identity of Old Irish *athir* and Sanskrit *pitā* 'father,' although they have not a single phoneme in common; for the differences accord with recognized phonetic laws. As wide a divergence in meaning can be traced only in case we have historic records of intermediate stages. One might well doubt the relationship of English *write* with Dutch *rijten* and German *reissen* 'tear, split,' if it were not for such intermediate stages as Old Saxon *wrītan* 'cut; write' and Icelandic *rīta* 'scratch; write.' No one knows whether Latin *ruō* 'fall' and *ruō* 'rush' are related or not, for we have no record of earlier Latin which might show either greater similarity between their meanings or greater divergence.

SHIFT OF SEMANTIC EMPHASIS

192. The meaning of a word varies with its context (*Johnny's a good reader: Johnny's in the third reader*); *Johnny's a good reader* means one thing in a first-grade schoolroom but quite another in a fifth-grade schoolroom or in a school of declamation. Similarly a given linguistic form will call forth different responses from different hearers; a description of good food may make a healthy, hungry man say "splendid!" while a dyspeptic may say "how unpleasant!" and one who has just eaten may say nothing at all. The word *goldenrod* means one thing to an artist, another to a careful farmer, and still another to a hay-fever patient. The word *shoe* tends to mean one thing to a laborer, or to a soldier, and something quite different to a dancer; one thing to a man and another to a woman; one thing to a mender of shoes and another to the owner of a shoe factory, or to the operator of shoe-making machinery, or to a retail salesman. But these nuances of meaning are not confined to any one of the classes named. Farmers and victims of hay fever may look at goldenrod in the artistic way. Soldiers or laborers may observe the shoes of a professional dancer. Some men may be as much interested in women's shoes as the women themselves.

If I am away from home and at last learn the date of my return, I may write my wife either *I'm coming home* or *I'm going home* on such and such a day. The English language permits me to make the statement either from her point of view or from my own. No wonder, then, that from the one Indo-European root *gwem-,* Sanskrit *gacchati* and Greek *bainei* mean 'he goes,' while Latin *venit* and English *comes* both suggest motion toward the speaker.

Latin *vēnditō* means 'offer for sale, try to sell,' often by praising one's wares. So, with shift of emphasis, Cicero (ad Atticum, 1. 16. 16) says to his friend Atticus, *valdē tē vēnditāvī,* 'I praised you a lot.' English *knave* is the same word as German *Knabe,* and its original meaning was 'boy.' Many boys were servants, and emphasis on that gave the word a new meaning; the transition stage is seen in Ancren Riwle, l. 380 (Morton): *þe kokes knaue, þet wasshed þe disshes.* Some servants are rascals, and emphasis upon that part of the idea gives the present-day meaning of *knave.*

193. The original meaning of English *dress* was the same as that of French *dresser* 'make straight,' and we still retain this in *dress ranks* and *dress timber.* The latter phrase implies the cutting away of surplus material, and, with emphasis upon this part of the idea, we get *dress hides, dress poultry, dress a vine.* In all these phrases the verb connotes preparation, and this is the preponderant feature in *dress a salad, dress a wound, dress the hair.* In this last phrase, and to a lesser degree in some of the others, there is an idea of adornment, which becomes emphatic in *dress a shop window* or *he dresses his wife well.* The latter involves clothing, and so finally we get such phrases as *dress one's self.*

On a bright summer's morning one doesn't say, *The sun is doubtless shining;* but on a rainy morning an airplane pilot may say, *At 10,000 feet the sun is doubtless shining.* The word is scarcely used unless some persons have doubts in the matter; it has come to mean virtually *'I'm sure although some are not.'*

194. Changes in culture may make a particular nuance of meaning more important than hitherto. *Pilot* in its older meaning involves the suggestion of detailed knowledge of the geography of a particular harbor; an airplane pilot need know nothing of the position of deep channels and shoal waters, but he must know something about the position of mountain ranges and a great deal about the weather.

Political history is responsible for the change of meaning of Latin *praetor.* As agent noun from *prae-eō,* the word originally meant 'he who goes before,' and it was a title of the highest military and civil officer. This officer's functions were gradually changed to those of judge of a criminal court, and the predominant meaning of the word kept pace; hence the inconsistency in classical Latin between *praetor* 'criminal judge' and *praetōrium* 'general's tent' or *nāvis praetōria* 'flagship.'

195. In addition to their intellectual content words suggest certain emotions. The chief difference in meaning between English *house* and *home* is of this sort; hence real-estate dealers offer for sale *a nice five-room home,* even though no one has yet lived in it. Sometimes the emphasis upon the emotional content of a word becomes so great that everything else is lost from sight. Intense dislike of *anarchists* and *socialists* leads many to couple the two words, as if they applied alike to all undesirable citizens, although anarchy and socialism are opposite extremes of political theory.

SHIFTERS

196. When I was a child, a neighbor once called to me as I was playing in the yard, "Is Mr. Sturtevant at home?" There were two men of that name living in our house, my grandfather and my father, so I said, "Do you mean the old man or the young man?" He reported to the household that I had called my father a *young man,* and I didn't hear the last of it for many months; but I was quite right, nevertheless; *old* and *young* are relative terms, and any father and son may be so described. Other words that constantly take their color from the context are *big little, high low, fast slow,* any terms that may imply measurements. A character in a recent novel, whose scene is set in the middle of the nineteenth century, expresses fear of the unreasonable speed of the new-fangled railway trains—sixteen miles an hour!

The extreme examples of words which get their meaning from the context are such adverbs as *here there, now then, up down,* and the personal pronouns, *I, you, he.* The only reason why any speakers can manage them successfully is that we have so very much practice.

SHIFT OF SEMANTIC EMPHASIS IN SYNTAX

197. In classical Latin *habeō* with the perfect participle usually keeps its full meaning; *Caesar aciem īnstrūctam habet* means 'Caesar keeps the battle line drawn up.' In Plautus, Pseudolus, 602, however, *illa omnia missa habeō* means 'I've dropped all that,' and this weakened meaning of *habēre* lies at the basis of the compound preterit of the Romance languages (e.g., French *j'ai envoyé* 'I sent'). The same development has occurred in English *I have lost,* in German *ich habe verloren,* in modern Greek *echo chameno.*

198. A number of Latin conjunctions have originated in just this way. The original meaning of *quamvīs* appears in Plautus, Menaechmi, 318: *Quamvīs rīdiculus est, ubi uxor non adest,* 'he's as funny as you please, when his wife isn't there.' The fully developed conjunction (subjunctive mood, and *tamen* in the main clause) appears in Cicero, ad Familiares, 7. 32. 3: *Illa quamvīs rīdicula essent, sīcut erant, mihi tamen rīsum nōn mōvērunt,* 'however funny those things were, as they really were, nevertheless they didn't make me laugh.' *Licet* 'it is permitted,' has become a conjunction in much the same way; Cicero, De Oratore, 1. 195: *Fremant omnēs licet, dīcam quod sentiō;* 'though all men grumble, I shall say what I think.' Ovid, Metamorphoses, 15. 62: *Isque, licet caelī regiōne remōtōs, mente deōs adiit,* 'he approached the gods in spirit, though they are far away in heaven's domain.'

INCLUSIVENESS

199. There are two ways of completely defining the meaning of a word: description and listing. One may easily describe the *moon* so fully that no one can doubt what object is meant, or one may point to the moon in the sky. If the word to be treated is *star,* the description will have to be more careful, or some stars (e.g., double stars, or dark stars) will be omitted; and the task of listing all stars will be enormous. Nevertheless there are always the two possible approaches to such a problem; to tell the content, the denotation of the word itself, or to indicate the range of its applicability, its inclusion.

If we define a *chair* as a seat with a back, intended for one person to sit on, then the word includes a majority of the pieces of furniture upon which we sit, but not *stools* (which have no backs) or *sofas, settees, benches,* etc. (which are intended for two or more occupants). The word *seat,* on the other hand, includes all the articles mentioned above; it may be defined as whatever people are expected to sit on.

When English *pen* shifted from the meaning 'feather used to write with' to 'writing instrument,' the word lost part of its denotation and consequently applied to more objects, had a wider inclusiveness. Greek *oinochoeuei* etymologically means *'is a wine-pourer, pours wine'*; when Homer makes Hebe 'wine-pour' nectar, the drink of the gods, he gives the verb less denotation and a wider inclusiveness. Similarly Latin *aedificāre* 'be a house-builder,' is freely used of building ships, towns, etc.

On the other hand English *animal* normally applies to all living things except plants, but sometimes has more denotation and far narrower inclusiveness, e.g.,*This powder destroys all insects, but is harmless to animal life.* Again the word may exclude humanity, as in the phrase *man and the animals.* A Florida law once forbade teaching that *man is a blood-relation of any animal.*

FIGURES OF SPEECH

200. In case of shift of semantic emphasis the change in denotation is the primary phenomenon, the change in inclusion is a corollary. Somctimes, however, a speaker intentionally makes a word include more territory (apply to a new object or class), and thereby necessarily deprives it of part of its denotation. The astronomer who first spoke of Jupiter's *moons* was applying the word to a new set of objects; he was increasing its inclusion. Thereby he decreased its denotation from 'the earth's satellite' to 'satellite.' The speaker who first called the support of a table a *leg* must have been aware that he was applying the word to a thing very different from what it had hitherto signified; one result was that *leg,* in its new use, immediately lost some of its content. Such a conscious and arbitrary extension of the applicability of a word is called a figure of speech.

It is often impossible to distinguish between semantic changes due to shift of emphasis and figures of speech. A four-year-old saw a blanket on a horse and called it an *apron*. Did he suppose that *apron* meant 'outer covering not always worn,' or did he mean to say, 'The horse is like a woman with an apron on'? Some of the following examples may belong under the head of Shift of Semantic Emphasis.

Figures of speech are used for suggestiveness or for clearness. We call a man an *ass* or we call him *sour* to arouse the emotions associated with the literal meanings of these words. A figurative expression contributes to clearness when a language lacks a literal word, as when we speak of a *transparent character*.

Faded **metaphors** are common in all languages. The word *clear* in *a clear statement* no longer suggests *clear water, a clear sky,* and the like. The *iris* of the eye was once the 'rainbow' of the eye. *Tulip* originally meant 'turban.' *Daisy* is properly *day's eye,* and was applied first to the sun and then, by a second metaphor, to the flower. The machine names *crane* and *gooseneck* preserve clear evidence of their etymologies.

There is a tendency to use concrete terms for abstract ideas; some intellectual processes are known by words of physical action. *To compose a poem* is *to put it together.* In *to get hold* of an idea the metaphor still lives, but not in *to comprehend*. Other such words are *simple,* which originally meant 'without fold'; *right,* originally 'straight'; *hard,* in such phrases as *a hard task, a hard man.*

Terms belonging to the sphere of one sense are often applied to the objects of another. In *loud colors* the metaphor is still alive; but a *sharp tongue* and a *high note* hardly suggest a comparison any longer.

Metonomy is the use of one word for another with which its meaning is closely connected, as when we say that a man sets a *good table* and keeps a *good cellar*. The fading of metonomy gives us *board* 'regular meals,' the *pulpit* meaning 'the clergy,' the *bar* for 'the lawyers,' a *chair* for 'a professorship.' Similarly Plato's school was named the *Academy* from the grove of Acadēmus, where they met.

Synecdoche is the naming of a thing from one of its parts or qualities. A part is used for the whole in *hands* for 'laborers,' a *blade* for a 'sword,' German *Bein* for 'leg.' Similarly, quality nouns often become collective nouns; English *youth* 'youngness' comes to mean 'those who are young.' Latin *multitūdō* 'maniness' came to mean 'a crowd.' A judge is called from a characteristic *your honor* and a king *your majesty.*

201. We often lack the data to decide whether a particular change of meaning is an instance of shift of semantic emphasis or a figure of speech. Many a child annoys his mother by calling various men *papa,* but no child has yet furnished convincing evidence of what he meant by the name. We can show clearly enough that Greek *thȳmos* 'life, emotion' had previously meant 'smoke, vapor,' that, in fact, it is the same word as Latin *fūmus* and Sanskrit *dhūmas* 'smoke, fume.' We can cite parallels for this change of meaning (Latin *animus* 'soul' beside Greek *anemos* 'wind'; Latin *spīritus* 'spirit' beside *spīrō* 'breathe'); but we have no evidence at all upon the way in which such changes occur.

ABBREVIATED PHRASES

202. Whenever one needs an expression which is more specific—that is, contains more information and applies to fewer objects—than any word in his language, he is compelled to use several words. This is the reason why we have adjectives and adverbs; there is no single word for *red light, large apple, six inches, sing sweetly,* and therefore we use phrases. Under ordinary circumstances such phrases serve us very well; but at any moment a group of speakers may come to use a particular phrase more frequently than is convenient. Among automobile drivers, for instance, the phrases *red light* and *green light* are something of a nuisance, and they are frequently abbreviated to *red* and *green* (he got a *red,* but presently crossed on the *green.*) An *electric light bulb* was at first one of many kinds of metal or glass protuberances, but in the 1880's it became very common; from that time on the phrase has often been abbreviated when the context makes the meaning clear.

In Roman military narrative *hīberna* is to be understood as representing *hīberna castra* 'winter quarters'; the number and gender must have reminded all speakers of the omitted noun. Similar in origin are English *moment* from *mōmentum temporis* 'movement of time' and *sermon* from *sermō religiōsus* 'religious conversation.' In the same way Horace repeatedy omits *vīnum* 'wine' when speaking of kinds of wine (*Massicum, Falernum, Caecubum*) we also speak of *Champagne, Madeira,* etc., without the word *wine.* In English *not* and German *nicht* the strengthened negative yields a single word (Old English *nāwight*), but in French the old negative and the strengthener are kept apart by word order (*je ne sais pas,* 'I don't know,' *il ne m'est rien* 'he's nothing to me'). Nevertheless abbreviation of the dissyllabic phrase has occurred; one commonly hears on the streets of Paris *je sais pas, il m'est rien.*

PLEONASM REDUCES DENOTATION

203. A speaker frequently says something twice; a young girl expresses her abounding good spirits by saying that she has *a grand and glorious feeling,* or one emphasizes his refusal by some sort of double negative (*No! not on your life!*). Frequently a pleonastic phrase shears a word of part of its meaning; a preacher once announced, *an afternoon service will be substituted instead,* where there is no meaning left for *substituted* but *held.* Livy, 21.32.7 writes: *fāmā prius . . . praecepta rēs erat,* 'the matter had been previously anticipated by rumor,' where *praecepta* has no meaning left but 'taken up.'

English *with* formerly meant 'against,' as it still does in a few phrases like *withstand* and *withhold,* and as the cognate *wider* does in German. In the phrase *fight with* the opposition was fully expressed by the verb, and only accompaniment was left for the preposition.

A good many Hellenistic decrees provide *stephanōsai basileā stephanōi chrysōi* 'to crown the king with a golden crown,' where the verb can mean only 'to honor.' Hence we read *stephanōsai basileā Attalon eiconi chalceāi* 'to honor king Attalos with a bronze statue.'

In Proto-Indo-European the accusative was used to denote end of motion, as in Latin *domum it.* The accusative, however, had other uses also, and the function of the case might be made clearer by an accompanying adverb of direction; thus (to use Latin forms) *virum eō* became *virum ad eō* 'to the man I go toward.' In the latter sentence the relation between verb and noun is fully expressed by *ad,* and there is left for *virum* only the fact that it depends upon *ad;* in other words *ad* has become a preposition. In Proto-Indo-European and also in the earliest Sanskrit and Greek, the words that are commonly called prepositions are somewhat like the German adverb *hinauf* in *er stieg den Berg hinauf,* while the fully developed prepositions of later times are more like English *up* in *he climbed up the mountain.* Even in Latin such a pair of sentences as *flūmen ineō* and *in flūmen eō* 'I enter the river,' shows that we are but one step removed from the use of *in* as an adverb; the position of the word has scarcely been fixed.

The same process weakens the personal forms of verbs until they must have a subject expressed. Latin *respondit* meant 'he replies.' It was possible, however, to add a pronominal subject, such as *is* or *ille;* and the pleonasm finally deprived the verb form of its personal force. Hence in French one must have *il répondit* for 'he replies.'

CHAPTER XIV

BORROWING

204. So far we have usually confined our attention to single languages, as if each of these had developed by itself. As a matter of fact, every known language has been largely influenced by its neighbors, through bilingual speakers; any man who uses two languages is sure to confuse them, especially at the points where they do not precisely correspond. The English vocabulary has been enormously enlarged by loans from various foreign languages.

205. Before the English language was brought to England it had been given a number of Latin words, including *wine* from Latin *vīnum* and *street* from Latin (*via*) *strāta*. Neither of these can have been taken over from Latin during the next period of contact, since at that time Latin *vīnum* had an initial [v] and *strāta* a [d] in the second syllable. English *street* also shows a prehistoric change of [a·] to [æ·]. They must both have been borrowed during the early Roman incursions into western Germany.

In the seventh century A.D. the Germanic peoples of England were converted to Christianity, and the Roman missionaries introduced several hundred Latin words into the language. The ecclesiastic *cirice* 'church' (Latin *cyriaca* from Greek *cyriacē*) and *biscop* 'bishop' (Latin *episcopus* had [b] in Vulgar Latin, as is shown by German *Bischof,* Portuguese *bispo,* etc.) were accompanied by many others, such as *plante* 'plant,' *regol* 'rule,' *fefor* 'fever,' and *munt* 'mount.' These words, as well as the earlier loans, were imposed upon the English language by the cultural superiority of the speakers of Latin, although many of the new terms displaced genuine English words.

206. In the period of the Danish invasions, the ninth to the eleventh centuries, a great many Scandinavian words were borrowed, such as *they, them, their, are* (where German has *sind*), *call, die, egg, hit, law, sister, wrong*. Noteworthy are the *sk*-words like *skirt* (beside genuine English *shirt*), *skin, sky*. A remarkable feature of these loans is the fact that they belong to the heart of the vocabulary, where borrowing is least likely to occur; the explanation is that, once the fighting was over, the speakers of Scandinavian were the rulers of northern England.

207. For some centuries after the Norman conquest, French was the first language of many Englishmen, and vast numbers of French words were naturalized. Every reader of Ivanhoe remembers how *swine, oxen,* and *calves* became *pork, beef,* and *veal* when served on the Norman nobleman's table. In many other fields also the English language presents a native word alongside a French word of nearly the same meaning; *yearly annual, hearty cordial, answer reply, body corpse, ghost spirit, room chamber, ship vessel, spring fountain.* Since French has ceased to be the language of the English aristocracy, loans from that source have become far less numerous, but there are still many of them.

In fact, throughout the contact with French, English borrowing has been on a scale that is characteristic of the socially inferior of two languages in contact; even to this day nothing is easier than for a French word to make its way among speakers of English. Bloomfield (p. 465) lists 100 extremely common French loan-words of such semantic spheres as government, law, war, religion, sport, architecture, the household, and personal names, words we could not do without. English words in French, on the other hand, are few and confined chiefly to sporting terms.

208. Ever since England became a maritime nation, and particularly since the establishment of English-speaking colonies in distant parts, words have been freely adopted from any language whatever. America's contributions include *igloo, moccasin, papoose, squaw, tomahawk, totem, wampum,* and *wigwam,* from Indian languages; *adobe, corral, mesa,* and *ranch,* from the Spanish of the southwest; *sauerkraut, smearcase, wienerwurst* or *wienies,* from German speakers in the large cities. Asia is represented by Chinese *tea, chow mein, shanghai;* Japanese *kimono, jin-riki-sha;* Malay *bamboo, gong, kampong* (often changed to *compound* by a popular etymology—§§ 170, 171), *orang-utan;* Dravidian *betel, calico, pariah;* Bengali *bungalow;* Hindi *jungle, punch,* and *toddy;* Persian *pagoda* and *shah;* Arabic *harem, koran, sherbet,* and *sultan;* Turkish *bey* and *kiosk*. Australia gives us *kangaroo* and *boomerang*. From Africa come *chimpanzee, gorilla, gnu,* and *zebra.*

209. Most of the words introduced into English by scholars, including translators, come from written languages, sometimes from modern languages, as *ablaut* and *umlaut* from German, but usually from Greek and Latin. These languages were brought to all the Mediterranean countries as conquerors' languages, and their use was long maintained by a large body of speakers, whose civilization was unquestionably higher than that of the subject peoples. Under such circumstances extensive borrowing is inevitable, and in this case the Latin language became the language of the church and of scholars throughout Western Europe. When scholars condescended to use the "vernacular languages," they naturally took over many Latin words, and, as these languages came by degrees to be the normal medium of scholarship, Latin continued to be the source from which new scholarly terms were taken. From ancient times Latin had contained many Greek words, and the greater freedom of composition in that language made it a convenient quarry from which to dig new scholarly terminology. From Latin, then, we have such words as *adjective, adverb, function, ictus,* and from Greek *arteriosclerosis, erysipelas, goniometric, thermodynamic.* In recent years the scientists have begun to save us the labor of learning such long words as these, instead they sometimes give us such short words as *ion, anion, cation, proton;* they even prefer the hybrid form *neutron* to a thoroughly Greek **ūdeter-on* for 'an uncharged, or neutral, particle.' The public also has taken a hand in naming the numerous recent discoveries; instead of *sulfanilamide, sulfapyridine, sulfathiazole* we may now say simply *sulfa* drugs.

210. A loan-word may have a long history and may travel over long distances. Our English word *gum* (in the phrases *chewing gum, gum elastic, gum tree,* etc.) is very widespread among the languages of Western Europe; it appears in Dutch *gom,* German, Swedish, and Danish *gummi,* French *gomme,* Portuguese and Italian *gomma,* Spanish *goma.* The word was borrowed by Middle English from Old French *gomme,* and it came into that language from Latin *gummis.* The latter word is evidently borrowed from Greek *commi,* whose earliest occurrence is in Herodotus' account of the embalming of human corpses by the Egyptians (2.86): *hypochriontes tōi commi, tōi dē anti collēs ta polla chreōntai Aigyptioi,* 'anointing [it] with *commi,* which the Egyptians generally use instead of glue.' We are told by Athenaeus, 2.66 f., that *commi* is a foreign word, and this statement is confirmed by the fact that it is indeclinable in Herodotus and variously declined elsewhere, and that it is quite without a Greek etymology. It seems safe, therefore, to assume that the word was borrowed from Egyptian by the Greeks. It is Egyptian *qmìt*,[1] Coptic *ḳomi* 'gum.'

BORROWING OF FORMATIVE ELEMENTS

211. When groups of words are borrowed they may be tied together by suffixes or prefixes. Thus, when the Latin-speaking Christians borrowed from the Greek *baptisma* 'baptism,' *baptista,* and *baptizō,* and also *evangelium* 'gospel,' *evangelista, evangelizō; sabbatum* 'sabbath,' *sabbatismus, sabbatizō; dogmaticus, dogmatistēs, dogmatizō,* they took over at the same time a number of Greek suffixes. These words were passed on to the French (*baptême, baptiste, baptiser; évangile, évangéliste, évangéliser; sabbat, sabbatisme; dogmatique, dogmatiste, dogmatiser*). The Norman French invaders carried these words to England, where they were reinforced by many parallel groups, which were not connected with the Christian religion. As a result of this bit of history we have a very active group of English suffixes, as follows:

general	———	———	*generalize*
commune	*communism*	*communist*	*communize*
theory	*theorism*	*theorist*	*theorize*
nude	*nudism*	*nudist*	———
union	*unionism*	*unionist*	*unionize*
American	*Americanism*	———	*Americanize*

The blank in the last line of the table may be filled by the word *Americanist* 'one who studies the culture of the American Indians'; but this word evidently has no connection with the other two derivatives, except that they are all three derivatives of the word *American,* in different meanings.

212. In the same way we have borrowed many Greek and Latin suffixes e.g., *-er* from Latin *-ārius* (*carpenter* from *carpentārius, usurer* from *ūsūrārius*) in such formations as *player, maker, old-timer, batter, tinner.* From the same source we have got the suffix *-ary,* in *apiary, coronary, epistolary, ordinary, pecuniary, primary, sanguinary, seminary,*

1. Erman and Gapow, Wörterbuch der aegyptischen Sprache, 5. 39.

capillary, exemplary. The compound suffix *-arian* comes in with loan-words like *vegetarian* (French *végétarien*), although we use it more widely than the French do (*sexagenarian* beside French *sexagénaire*).

213. The suffix *-ate,* with which we form verbs from Latin verbs of the first conjugation (*fascinate* from *fascināre, venerate* from *venerārī, orate* from *ōrāre*), has a rather complicated history. It was originally used to represent Latin nouns in *-ātus* (*tribunate, consulate, episcopate* 'bishopric'), and participial adjectives in *-ātus* (*sedate, ornate, accumulate*). Then, on the analogy of causative verbs like *to warm* (<Old English *wearmian*) beside the adjective *warm* and also of pairs like *to clear* (<Latin *clārāre*) beside *clear* (<Latin *clārus*), the adjectives *aggravate, separate,* etc., came to be used also as verbs. The suffix has tended to give way to *-ated* in its older participial use (*accumulated, aggravated, separated*), and it is now freely used to anglicize any first conjugation verb (*felicitate*) or any French verb in *-er* (*assassinate*). We even go further and make entirely new verbs with the suffix (*camphorate, substantiate.*)

TRANSLATION LOANS

214. Sometimes a foreign word is translated rather than borrowed. Oertel cites English *overdrive* and *overdriven* from a certain writer in the sense of 'exaggerate, exaggerated'; they evidently translate German *übertreiben* and *übertrieben*. English *aeroplane* has been supplanted by *airplane.* During the last hundred years or so strong efforts have been made to purify the German language of the burden of foreign elements by substituting *Kurzschrift* for *Stenographie, Eindecker* for *Monoplan, Vertrag* for *Kontrakt,* etc. This modern reform is in harmony with a tendency that has long existed; Goethe substituted *Wasserleitung* for *Aquaeduct, umlaufen* for *circulieren, Zwischenreich* for *Interregnum.*

Translators of the Bible are anxious to represent the exact force of the original and also to be understood. Loan-words would be exact, but only native speech material can be understood. Hence the Vulgate represents Greek *sympathō* by Latin *compatior, hyperecperissou* by *superabundanter, synoikō* by *cohabitō, synaichmalōtos* by *concaptīvus.* Since Christianity was carried to the Germans by the Roman Church, Latin words rather than Greek are reflected in the German technical terms of Christianity; *compatior* has yielded *mitleiden, compater* gives *Gevatter, cōnscientia* is reflected by *Gewissen.*

It is characteristic of English that we say *sympathy* where Germans say *Mitleid* and *conscience* for *Gewissen;* Jespersen (Language p. 215) says that "English differs from most European languages in having a much greater propensity to swallowing foreign words raw, as it were, than to translating them." Nevertheless the English Bible has *fellow-captive* for *concaptīvus* and *almighty* for *omnipotēns.*

PHONEMIC LOANS

215. Loan-words are generally pronounced according to the phonemic system of the borrowing language. English *pork* and *corpse* have the usual aspirated initial [pᶜ] and [kᶜ]. Nevertheless some effort is made to follow a foreign pronunciation; as when Romans undertook to imitate the Greek aspirates (§ 121), or when the French uvular *r* was introduced into Germany (§ 117). English has the phonemic group [ts] very commonly in final position (*pots, pits, feats, rats, roots, oats*), but it occurs initially only in a few loan-words, of which one alone is at all common, namely, *tsetse,* a Bantu name of the fly that carries the African sleeping sickness. Quite as rare in initial position is [pw], which nevertheless occurs commonly enough in Spanish *pueblo,* and in a few other loan-words, such as *Pwyll,* the name of a Cymric god. Another such initial group is *tm* in *tmesis,* the name of Mt. *Tmolus,* and several even rarer words.

216. The introduction of foreign phonemes is very common, of course, whenever an adult learns a new language. This is the familiar situation of hosts of American immigrants who speak English with a "foreign accent." Under the conditions prevailing here, it is certain that foreign phonemes introduced in this way will usually disappear in the speech of the second or third generation (cf. § 110).

BORROWING AT HOME

217. So far we have been considering loans from one language to another; we have found these most frequent between neighboring languages as French and English, but they may occur between any two languages in the world. We must now observe the far more common but less striking process by which speakers of neighboring local or class dialects influence one another.

It is quite impossible to register all such dialects; in fact it may be said that each speaker has a special dialect of his own, since his friends can recognize him by his speech. The members of a household often have certain linguistic habits in common, and so do the members of each craft or other occupation; say, the housewives (*a felled seam*), the printers (*a galley proof*), the carpenters (*a jack plane*). Of course it is impossible to define the membership of any such class precisely; the housewives' dialect is shared in part with the tailors, and in another part with the cooks; the printers' dialect with the editors and in part with the authors. Furthermore all these groups are in constant communication with the other groups; they are sure to influence one another's speech all the time. And just so cross influences between the dialects of neighboring villages or other regions are extremely frequent. In a country where travel is as active as it is in the United States such inter-dialectal borrowings are facilitated by the dislocation of dialect speakers. A few illustrations may be in order.

During my first thirty years I always pronounced *trough* [trɔθ], and supposed that to be the universal pronunciation. Then I saw the word in a printed list of words having *gh* for *f*. I recorded this error of mine in Linguistic Change, p. 34, along with the comment that I could not have made it if the word had not had an ambiguous spelling. In due course an aunt, who had been a member of my father's family during my childhood, read this passage and exclaimed: "Why! I always say troth!" I promptly assumed that I had learned the word from her. But Map 208 in the Linguistic Atlas of New England shows that [θ] is the usual final consonant of *trough* in Connecticut, whence my father's family migrated to Illinois, and that the same final consonant prevails in southwestern Maine, where my mother spent her childhood. Probably in my early years I never heard any other pronunciation than [trɔθ]. According to the most recent Webster, "the dialectal pronunciation *troth* is widespread in America, and known in England."

Postvocalic *r* has been lost in London and vicinity, but it is retained in most of the rural English counties. Both treatments were evidently brought to the United States by the early settlers, and their redistribution is still going on.[2] In general postvocalic *r* has been lost in eastern New England except in eastern Maine, Essex and Plymouth Counties in Massachusetts, Martha's Vineyard, and Nantucket. It is prevalent in western New England. In the Connecticut valley the two pronunciations are in conflict, one gaining in one town and the other in another town. The Old South is generally free from postvocalic *r* except for a district along the coast between Charleston, S.C., and Wilmington, N.C.; eastern Maryland; and the mountains, including all of West Virginia. The native speech of the City of New York lacks postvocalic *r*, and so does that of neighboring Jersey City and Newark. Philadelphia is the only important Atlantic port to retain the sound. Kurath points out that Colonial American merchants and bankers maintained close relations with London, and sent their sons there for their apprenticeship. Furthermore the sons of Southern planters were often educated in Oxford or Cambridge. Such practices doubtless did a great deal to strengthen the prestige of the London dialect in the American seaports and in the cotton and tobacco regions of the South. One wonders why Philadelphia did not fall in line with the other harbor towns; did the Quaker youth purposely guard their *r*'s while working in London?

These illustrations show how the American migrations have confused the inheritance of dialect features in this country. In fact there are very few local differences in the speech of the United States that do not have parallels in England, but they are differently combined on the two sides of the ocean.

218. We do not know of any such thorough-going change of population in the history of Europe. There we have usually a conquest by a relatively small number of invaders and the establishment of a government of occupation. This has often resulted in a change of language (Latin for Celtic in France; English for Celtic in England; German for Slavic east of the Oder); and no doubt it has been accompanied by some confusion of preëxisting dialect distinctions; but the important linguistic process must always have been the learning of a new language by relatively large numbers of the vanquished.

Nevertheless dialect features must have tended to spread by imitation

2. Bernard Bloch gave a report on the situation in New England in Actes du quatrième congrès international de linguistes, pp. 195–199, Copenhagen (1938).

throughout the Latin-speaking territory and the Germanic-speaking territory as long as these remained unbroken. The details of the process within recent years can be followed by the study of dialect atlases, and

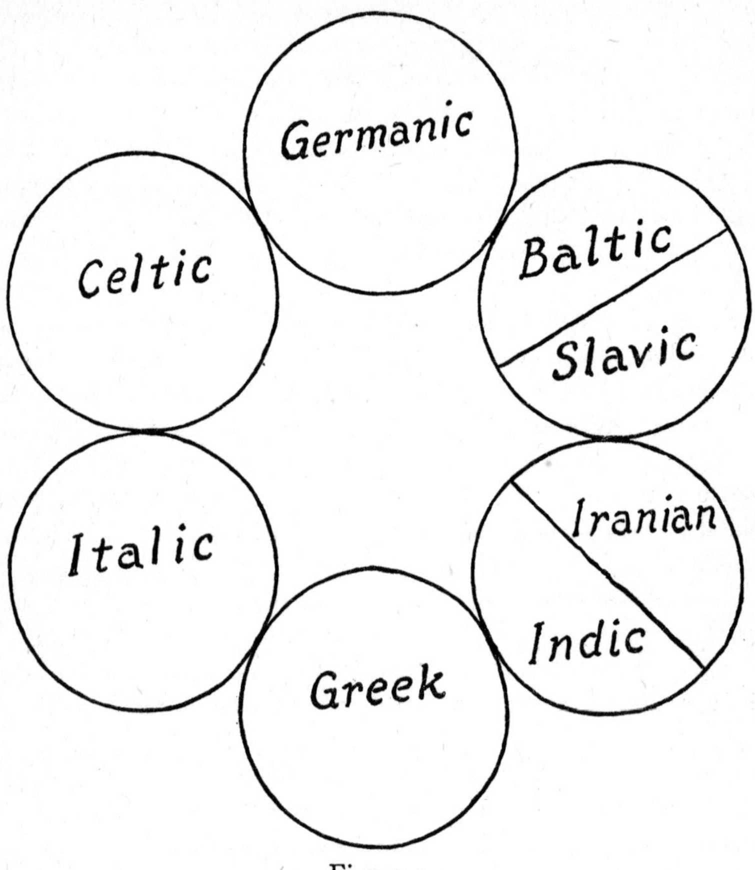

Figure 4.

Prehistoric distribution of the Indo-European languages, as implied by Johannes Schmidt.

more and more skill is being developed in tracing the similar processes of earlier times.

219. Long ago the view was expressed[3] by Johannes Schmidt that similar spread of linguistic features between the several Indo-European

3. Johannes Schmidt, Die Verwandtschaftsverhältnisse der indogermanischen Sprachen (1872).

languages can be detected. His discussion concerned Germanic, Balto-Slavic, Iranian-Indic, Greek, Italic, and Celtic, and tended to show that these six groups formed a ring in this order; identical characteristics,

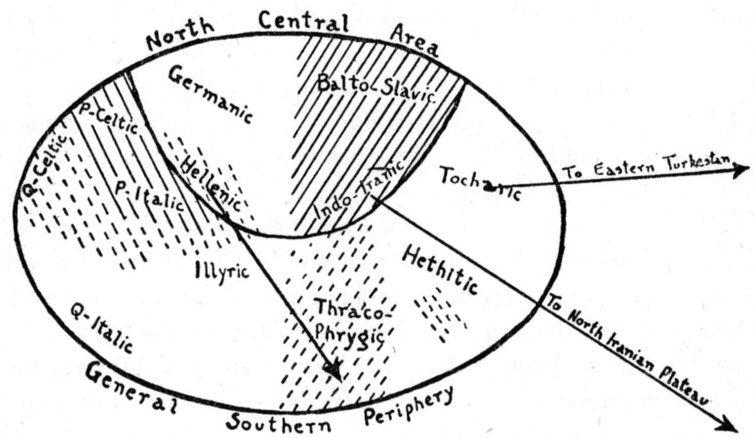

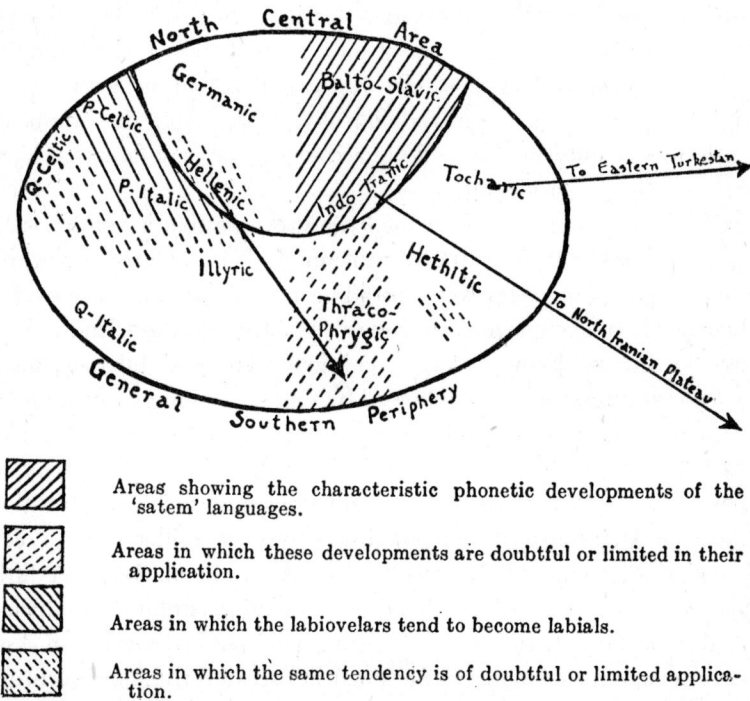

Areas showing the characteristic phonetic developments of the 'satem' languages.

Areas in which these developments are doubtful or limited in their application.

Areas in which the labiovelars tend to become labials.

Areas in which the same tendency is of doubtful or limited application.

The arrows show later movements whereby earlier contacts were disrupted.

Figure 5.

Prehistoric distribution of the Indo-European languages, according to Kerns and Schwartz.

whether phonemic, morphologic, or lexical, tend to be shared between Germanic and Balto-Slavic (especially Baltic), Balto-Slavic and Iranian-Indic (especially between Slavic and Iranian), Indic and Greek, Greek and Italic, Italic and Celtic, Celtic and Germanic. In a general way this corresponds with the geographical position of the languages at the dawn of history, when there were speakers of Iranian along the northern shore of the Black Sea. Schmidt argued, therefore, that the numerous features common to contiguous links in the chain had spread by borrowing.

The geographic neatness of Schmidt's ring of six linguistic communities (see Figure 4) was variously disturbed by the attempts of his successors to find room in the diagram for the other related languages. We select one of the most recent of these pseudo-maps (see Figure 5), the one published by J. Alexander Kerns and Benjamin Schwartz in 1937.[4] It is quite evident that the difficulty of preserving the simplicity of Schmidt's argument while taking account of the new facts that have come to light is considerable.

220. The real weakness of the theory, however, is that it assumes such conditions for the third or fourth millennium before Christ, when the Indo-European languages were spreading over the world, as prevailed while the Latin language spread over the Mediterranean lands. As a matter of fact we know that the conditions were very different; there were no far-flung conquests followed by thorough-going occupation by a great power. The best and clearest account we have of the kind of expedition undertaken then is in Chapters 2–29 of the first book of Caesar's Gallic War. The Helvetii undertook just such an expedition as had been customary among their relatives for millennia; it failed because Caesar blocked their path with the power of Rome. A little more than 200 years earlier a band of Celts under Brennus conducted a raid upon Greece, and some of them finally reached Galatia in Asia Minor, where their language continued in use until the fourth century A.D. During 600 years these Celts were completely out of touch with the speakers of closely related languages.

221. We know very little about the earlier migrations of speakers of Indo-European languages, but we know that in early times the speakers of Italic, Greek, and Indic were largely cut off from communication with the speakers of related languages.[5] We know less about the early history of other Indo-European speakers, but certainly they were all adventurous travelers and in contact with other men not very far removed from nomadic habits. We are not justified in thinking of a gradual expansion of a solid core of Indo-European speech. The spread of

4. Language, 13. 277 (1937).

5. Some speakers of Italic no doubt came into contact with speakers of Massapic, Venetic, Gaulish, and Greek, but for the most part these contacts were not close enough or early enough to influence the Latin language as Italian has been influenced by French.

the Latin language over the Mediterranean countries was a very different matter.

222. Furthermore we know of several types of Indo-European speech that, in ancient times, intervened between the languages of which we have records. Venetic was spoken in northeastern Italy, Messapic in southern Italy, Illyrian on the eastern shore of the Adriatic, Thracian about the northern end of the Aegean sea, Scythian to the north of the Black Sea. In Asia Minor were used a number of languages closely related to Indo-European (§ 235). These languages and several others that were not closely related to Indo-European fairly cover the territory about which we have fullest information from the classical authors.

If we assume a similar state of affairs elsewhere and earlier in the history of Indo-European, we must conclude that many types of Indo-European speech have perished quite without record. The languages of which we have early texts represent a set of distinct regional types.

223. The spread of the Indo-European languages must have occurred by means of a large number of greater or lesser forays. Caesar says the Helvetian expedition included 368,000 persons; if they had established themselves, say, in northern Spain, they might have introduced a Celtic language there as thoroughly isolated from other Celtic speech as was the Galatian of Asia Minor.

CHAPTER XV

THE COMPARATIVE METHOD

224. When a linguistic community breaks into several parts, either by long journeys of groups of speakers, or by their crossing mountain ranges or seas, or by the incursion of a foreign group in such a way as to form an effective barrier, and when this situation persists for many centuries, there arises the situation that enables scholars to carry on the kind of study that is called **comparative grammar.**

Comparative grammar reconstructs certain features of the language spoken by the original, unseparated community, on the basis of corresponding features of the descendent languages. If two of these show the same feature, this is, in general, more likely to have been inherited from the common ancestor of both languages than to have originated independently in the two descendent languages, unless they are known to have been subjected to some common influence. For example, Greek and Sanskrit [1] possess a verb form for 'he sits,' Greek *hēstai,* Sanskrit *āstē.* The Greek diphthong *ai* corresponds to Sanskrit *ē* in many other words (e.g., *hēntai : āsatē* 'they sit,' *pherontai : bharantē* 'they carry for themselves'). Furthermore both Greek *ai* and Sanskrit *ē* correspond to Latin *ae* in such words as Greek *aithō* 'I kindle' : Latin *aestus* 'heat,' Sanskrit *ēdhas* 'fire-wood' : Latin *aedēs* 'temple' (at first probably 'fire-place'); Greek *aiōn* : Latin *aevum* 'life-time.' The two medial consonants correspond in hosts of words (e.g., Greek *esti* : Sanskrit *asti* 'he is,' Greek *potnia* : Sanskrit *patnī* 'mistress, lady,' Greek *genos* : Sanskrit *janas* 'race'). Greek *ē* corresponds to Sanskrit *ā* in many words (e.g., Greek *tithēsi* : Sanskrit *dadhāti* 'he places,' Greek *hēmi-* : Sanskrit *sāmi-* 'half'). The initial *h* of Greek *hēstai* comes from the first person singular and plural, where *hēmai* and *hēmetha* developed regularly from ear-

1. The word occurs also in Avestan, but that fact may be disregarded here, since Avestan is so clearly related to Sanskrit that the two of them together must be counted as a single witness.

lier **ēhmai* and **ēhmetha* from **ēsmai* and **ēsmetha;*[2] cf. Greek *hīmeros* 'desire' : Sanskrit *Iṣmas,* a name of the god of love.

In the above discussion we have merely given reasons for concluding that Greek *hēstai* and Sanskrit *āstē* are both inherited from Proto-Indo-European; we have not tried to reconstruct the form of the word in the parent language. This task has, however, been undertaken. Greek *ai* : Sanskrit *ē* is traced by all scholars to Proto-Indo-European *ai.* Greek medial *st* = Sanskrit *st* indicates the same group in the parent language. Greek *ē* : Sanskrit *ā* is now held to represent Proto-Indo-European *ē,* although earlier scholars preferred to assume rather that Sanskrit *ā* was the original sound and that it had split, under unknown conditions, into *ē, ō,* and *ā* in certain European and West-Asiatic languages. Scholars now agree in assuming that Proto-Indo-European had a verb *ēstai* 'he sits.'

225. While all are agreed as to Proto-Indo-European *ēstai,* there is much more evidence on such a word as Sanskrit *pitā́,* Armenian *hair,* Greek *patḗr,* Latin *pater,* Old Irish *athir,* Gothic *fadar* 'father.' Here Sanskrit, together with other Indo-Iranian languages, differs from the related tongues in lacking a final *-r.* Since final *-r* survives in some words (e.g., *dadur* 'they gave' : Latin *dedēre*), we conclude that Proto-Indo-European also lacked the *r* under unknown conditions; we therefore set it in parentheses in our reconstruction.

Sanskrit and Greek agree as to the quantity of the vowel of the second syllable; as we have already noted (§ 224), Greek *ē* : Sanskrit *ā* indicates Proto-Indo-European *ē.* Armenian *hair* supports this conclusion, since *i* is the regular representative of Proto-Indo-European *ē* in that language (e.g., Armenian *mair* : Sanskrit *mātā,* Greek *mātēr*[3] 'mother'). In Latin the shortening of a long vowel before final *r* is regular (cf. passive *amor* beside active *amō* 'I love'). Gothic *fadar* also shows the regular Gothic development of final *-ēr.*

We have already seen (§ 224) that Proto-Indo-European *t* persists in Sanskrit and in Greek; it persists also in Latin (cf. *est* 'he is'; Sanskrit *trayas* : Latin *trēs* 'three'). In Armenian *t* between vowels becomes *y,* and then *y* is lost in certain circumstances (cf. *mair* 'mother'). In Old Irish *t* after a vowel becomes *th* (cf. *brathir* : Latin *frāter* 'brother').

2. Sommer, Griechische Lautstudien, p. 28 (1904); Hirt, Handbuch der griechischen Laut- und Formenlehre, 2d ed. p. 227 (1912).

3. This is the general Greek word. Attic-Ionic *mētēr* has the regular change of *ā* to *ē.*

Gothic *fadar* shows *d* [ð] instead of þ [θ], which is the usual Gothic resultant from Proto-Indo-European *t* (cf. *þrija*: Latin *tria* 'three'). In pre-Germanic (§ 228) *þ* became *d* [ð] if immediately preceded by a vowel unaccented in Proto-Indo-European. At the same time other spirants also became voiced in this position, which must mean that the pre-Germanic accent rested upon the same syllables as in Proto-Indo-European.

The vowel of the first syllable of the word for 'father' is *a* in all the languages cited above except Sanskrit, where the vowel is *i*. The same situation exists in a good many other words (e.g., Sanskrit *sthitas* : Greek *statos,* Latin *status* 'standing'; Sanskrit *duhitā*: Greek *thygatēr* 'daughter'; Sanskrit *kravis*: Greek *creas* 'raw flesh'); but very often Sanskrit shows *a* beside *a* in the other languages (e.g., *ajāmi*: Greek *agō,* Latin *agō* 'I lead, drive'; *ajras* : Greek *agros,* Latin *ager,* Gothic *akrs* 'field'; *apa*: Greek *apo,* Latin *ab,* Gothic *af* 'from'). Most scholars assume two separate phonemes in Proto-Indo-European, *a,* which remains in all the language groups, and *ə,* which becomes *i* in Indo-Iranian and *a* in other groups. We write *ə* in our reconstruction of the Proto-Indo-European word for 'father.'

The initial consonant of the word for 'father' is *p* in Sanskrit, Greek, and Latin. The Armenian change of Proto-Indo-European *p* to *h* is paralleled in a number of words (*hing*: Sanskrit *panca,* Greek *pente* 'five'; *hem*: Sanskrit *parut,* Greek *perusi* 'last year'). In Old Irish, as in the other Celtic languages, initial *p* is lost regularly (e.g., *orc*: Latin *porcus* 'pig'; *ro,* an intensive particle, : Sanskrit *pra,* Greek *pro* 'before'). Gothic and the other Germanic languages present many parallels to the change of Proto-Indo-European initial *p* to *f* (e.g., *fimf*: Sanskrit *panca,* Greek *pente* 'five'; *fisks*: Latin *piscis* 'fish').

Only three of the words cited above contain evidence on the accent of the Proto-Indo-European word for 'father'; the Sanskrit, the Greek, and the Gothic. The recorded accent of the Sanskrit and Greek words is on the last syllable, and the existence of *d* instead of *þ* at the beginning of the second syllable in Gothic confirms the conclusion. We therefore reconstruct the Proto-Indo-European word for 'father' as *pətḗ(r)*.

226. Without stating the detailed argument for each phoneme involved we may list the Sanskrit, Greek, Latin, and Gothic words upon which we base the reconstruction of the first ten numerals of Proto-Indo-European.

Sanskrit	Greek	Latin	Gothic	Proto-Indo-European
	oinē 'ace'	ūnus	ains	oinos
duā, dvā	dyō, dōdeca	duo	twa	duō, dwō
trayas	treis	trēs	þreis	treyes
catvāras	tettares	quattuor	fidwor	kwetwōres
panca	pente	quīnque	fimf	penkwe
ṣaṭ	hex	sex	saiks	sek̂s
sapta	hepta	septem	sibun	septm̥
aṣṭau	octō	octō	ahtau	ok̑tōu
nava	ennea	novem	niun	newn̥
daśa	deca	decem	taihun	dek̂m̥

A good many phonetic laws are implied in this table. Some of them are quite obvious, e.g., Proto-Indo-European *oi* remains in Greek, becomes Latin *ū*, Gothic *ai*. Some of them had better be stated here: Proto-Indo-European *ă*, *ĕ*, *ŏ* all appear in Sanskrit as *ă*. Proto-Indo-European *āu*, *ēu*, *ōu* all appear in Sanskrit as *au*. Proto-Indo-European *m̥* and *n̥* yield Sanskrit and Greek *a;* Latin *em, en;* Gothic *um, un* (Latin **noven*—cf. *nōnus* 'ninth'—becomes *novem* by anticipation of *decem* (§ 130. 2); in Gothic final *m* becomes *n*). Proto-Indo-European *ḳw* before *e* becomes Sanskrit *c* and Greek *t*. Proto-Indo-European *k̂* (a fronted *ḳ*) usually appears in Sanskrit as a sibilant. In Latin initial *p* before *qu* of the next syllable becomes *qu*. Proto-Indo-European *w* is lost in Attic Greek. In Gothic, Proto-Indo-European *p, t, ḳ* become *f, þ, h,* but after an unaccented vowel *b, d, g;* Proto-Indo-European *d* becomes *t;* Proto-Indo-European *k̂t* becomes *ht*. The second *f* of Gothic *fimf* is due to lag (§ 131. 2). Too complicated to explain here are the following items : the two forms of 'two' in Sanskrit and Greek, Sanskrit *ṣaṭ,* the *-a-* of Greek *tettares,* the initial *en-* of Greek *ennea,* the *-att-* of Latin *quattuor*.

§ 227. On the basis of a great deal of evidence like this we have succeeded in constructing a family tree of the well-attested Indo-European languages, which starts as follows:

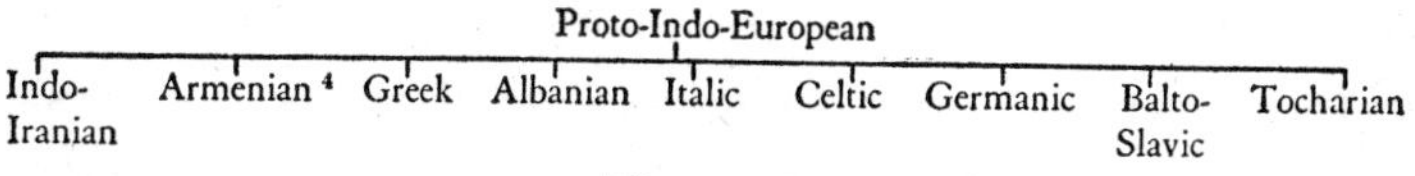

Proto-Indo-European

Indo-Iranian | Armenian[4] | Greek | Albanian | Italic | Celtic | Germanic | Balto-Slavic | Tocharian

Figure 6.

4. But see Austin, Language 18. 22–25 (1942).

This diagram does not indicate in what order the several languages were removed from the parent stock. It does not mean, either, that all the migrations by which the Indo-European languages were spread over a large part of the Eastern Continent took place at approximately the same time. Many efforts have been made to determine the order in which the several groups separated, but, in my opinion, none of them have been successful. The placing of all nine groups in the same line is, therefore, a mark of ignorance; it does not amount to an assertion that they all broke away at about the same time.

228. By way of example we may give the extension of the diagram as far as it concerns the Germanic languages:

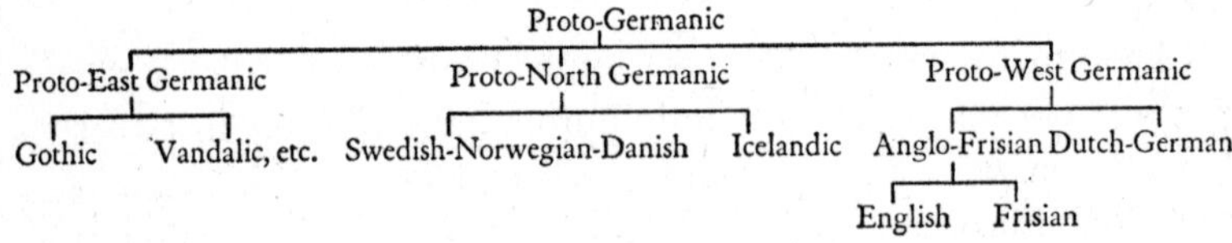

Figure 7.

On the basis of the relationships here suggested scholars reconstruct in part the Proto-Germanic language; its word for 'father' is set up as *fader,* which differs from the corresponding Gothic word only in the vowel of the final syllable. We have noticed (§ 225) that a period called pre-Germanic intervened between the linguistic stage known as Proto-Indo-European and the one known as Proto-Germanic. It was during this period that voiceless spirants became voiced after unaccented vowels, before the inherited accent was shifted to the initial syllable.

It is also possible to reconstruct Proto-West Germanic by comparing English, Frisian, and Dutch-German. The Proto-West Germanic word for 'father' was *fader*.

229. Early in the present century extensive documents in the Hittite language were discovered in northeastern Asia Minor. Their interpretation and their close relationship to Indo-European were announced by Bedrich Hrozný in December, 1915. In spite of the difficulties presented by the first World War, Hrozný published his grammar only two years later.[5] Hrozný was not an Indo-Europeanist, and he presented his

5. Die Sprache der Hethiter, ihr Bau und ihre Zugehörigkeit zum indogermanischen Sprachstamm; ein Entzifferungsversuch, Leipzig, 1917.

argument rather inexpertly; furthermore, the material upon which the argument was based had not yet been published. Consequently he was not generally believed for some years, although he actually proved his case at the start.

230. The Hittite documents are written in a form of the cuneiform syllabary which neglects the distinction between voiced and voiceless phonemes; we have learned now that double writing of *tt, pp, ḳḳ,* or *ḫḫ* shows that the phoneme indicated is voiceless, but in many positions the syllabary makes such a writing impossible, and it seems to have been optional in any case. Furthermore we often meet other consonants than these four written double (namely, *zz, mm, nn, ll, rr,* and *ss*). There is no proof that the double writing of these denotes voicelessness. In this book the doubling of the first four will be interpreted as follows: *tt* = *t*, *pp* = *p*, *ḳḳ* = *ḳ*, *ḫḫ* = *x*; but the singly written *t, p, ḳ,* and *ḫ* will be interpreted as *t* or *d*, *p* or *b*, *ḳ* or *g*, *x* or *γ* as seems probable on etymological or other grounds. Both *z* and *zz* will be transcribed *ts,* and the other groups will be rendered *m, n, l, r,* and *s*.

231. The close connection of the language with the Indo-European languages is in part proved as follows. The declension of the personal nouns runs, nominative *-s,* accusative *-n,* genitive *-as,* dative *-i,* instrumental *-t,* ablative *-ts,* nominative plural *-es*. Neuters, aside from a few original *o*-stems, show the bare stem in nominative and accusative singular. Peculiarly striking are the numerous neuter stems with nominative-accusative singular in *-r* and all other cases in *-n-* (e.g., *wadar,* genitive *wedenas* 'water').

The presents of the first conjugation end in first person *-mi,* second *-si,* third *tsi,* first plural *-weni* or *-meni,* second plural *-teni,* third plural *-(a)ntsi*. The two third person forms show the regular change of inherited *ti* to *tsi*. Two illustrations are *edmi* 'I eat' *adanzi* 'they eat'; *esmi* 'I am' *estsi* 'he is' *asanzi* 'they are.'

Among the pronouns we must mention especially *ḳuis,* neuter *ḳuid,* plural *ḳues* 'who.'

Here are a few clear etymologies.

genu : Latin *genū* 'knee.'
gwentsi : Sanskrit *hanti* 'strikes, slays.'
gunantsi : Sanskrit *ghnanti* 'they strike, slay.'
luḳtsi 'kindles, grows light,' Latin *lūcet* 'makes light, shines.'

melit: Greek *meli melitos* 'honey,' Gothic *miliþ*.

nebes 'sky': Sanskrit *nabhas* 'sky, cloud,' Greek *nephos* 'cloud,' Church-Slavic *nebo* 'sky.'

newas: Sanskrit *navas,* Greek *neos,* Latin *novus* 'new.'

newaxtsi : Latin *novat* 'renews.'

neyantsi: Sanskrit *nayanti* 'they lead, conduct.'

padan 'place': Greek *pedon* 'ground, earth.'

septamas: Sanskrit *saptamas,* Latin *septimus* 'seventh.'

sestsi: Sanskrit *sasti* 'sleeps.'

tres: Sanskrit *trayas,* Greek *treis,* Latin *trēs,* Gothic *þreis* 'three.'

weḳtsi: Sanskrit *vaṣṭi* 'demands,' Greek *heḳōn* 'willing.'

yugan: Sanskrit *yugam,* Greek *zygon,* Latin *iugum,* Gothic *juḳ* 'yoke.'

232. In spite of this and much more evidence connecting Hittite with the Indo-European languages, the Hittite verbal system is remarkably unlike that of the older Indo-European languages (Sanskrit, Avestan, Greek, and Latin). The Hittite verb is conjugated in two voices (active and medio-passive), two moods (indicative and imperative), and two tenses (present-future and preterit), supplemented by several compound tenses like English *is gone, is done,* and *has made.*

For this reason and the observation of a number of archaisms in Hittite, Emil Forrer [6] suggested that Hittite broke away from the parent language before any of the other known Indo-European languages, and thus had a longer period of prehistoric development than Sanskrit, Greek, or Latin. I adopted this suggestion and have argued for it a number of times; my fullest statement of the case, together with references to opposing arguments, appeared in 1942.[7]

233. Hittite has a system of sentence connectives including the particles *ta, su,* and *nu.* Adelaide Hahn [8] notes that in nearly all occurrences in the Law Code *ta* introduces a clause of subsequent action; it may have

6. Mitteilungen der deutschen Orient-Gesellschaft, 61. 26 f. (1921).

7. The Indo-Hittite Laryngeals, pp. 23–28, Baltimore (1942); with this should be combined Journal of the American Oriental Society, 47. 174–177 (1927), and Language, 15. 11–19 (1939). A number of scholars remain unconvinced, notably Holger Pedersen, Hittitisch und die anderen indoeuropäischen Sprachen, Copenhagen (1938), Tocharisch vom Gesichtspunkt der indoeuropäischen Sprachvergleichung, pp. 4 f., Copenhagen (1941); and Giuliano Bonfante, Indogermanische, Forschungen, 52. 221–226 (1934), Revue belge de philologie et d'histoire, 18. 381–392 (1939), Classical Philology, 39. 51–57 (1944), 40. 116–121 (1945), American Journal of Philology, 67. 289–310 (1946).

8. Language, 12. 108 f. (1936).

meant 'afterwards, next' or the like. Holger Pedersen [9] finds a meaning 'deshalb' for Hittite *su,* but I can see nothing in it but a connective. Hittite also has an enclitic pronoun equivalent to Latin *is,* which is confined to the nominative and accusative, singular and plural; it shows the forms *-as, -an, at;* plural *-e, -us, -as, -e -a.* This is freely appended to the first word of a sentence (*man-as* 'if he,' *nama-an* 'then him,' *amuk-at* 'I it'), and is very frequently combined with the sentence connectives (*tas, tan, tat; sas, san; nas, nan, nat*). Hrozný saw the connection of Hittite *tas tan tat* with Greek *ho ton to* and Sanskrit *sa tam tat,* but he did not notice how similar to Hittite usage are some passages in Homer, in the earliest Sanskrit prose, and in early Germanic prose. In Iliad, 1. 53–58 we have at the beginning of four clauses *tēi, tōi, hoi,* and *toisi;* no man can prove that these words are connectives, since they are all accompanied by *de* or *gar,* but it is a plausible theory that the tendency of the "article" to stand at the head of its clause is a trace of its original use as a connective. This is even clearer in the "relative article"; Iliad, 1. 234 f.; *nai ma tode scēptron, to men ou pote phylla cai ozous physei* may be translated, 'By this scepter; and it will never put forth leaves and twigs.'

In the following translation of a few lines from the Çatapatha-Brāhmana, 1. 8. 1. 5 the words that translate forms of our pronoun are italicized. A certain fish had promised Manu that if he reared it until it was strong he would be saved from a flood. '*And it* having thus reared he carried to the sea. *And it* what year *from then* had indicated, *in that* year by fitting out a ship he followed the advice. *And he,* when the flood came, boarded the ship. *And to him that* fish swam. *And* to *its* horn the ship's painter he attached. *And by it* he ran to that northern mountain.' With this should be compared a translation of a few lines from the inaugural address of Hattusilis III,[10] where the translations of forms of *nas* are italicized. 'And I shut the enemy in Hahha. *And him* I fought. And me Ištar, my Lady, helped. *And him* I smote. And I got the upper hand. But whatever Hittite he had with him, *him* I excepted. *And him,* every one, I established again. The helpers, however, I took. *And them* I sent to my brother.'

9. Hittitisch und die anderen indoeuropäischen Sprachen, p. 196 (1938), Tocharisch, p. 5 (1941).

10. Goetze, Hattusilis = Sturtevant and Bechtel, Chrestomathy, Apology of Hattusilis, 2. 23–29.

A comparison of these passages and such a text as the Anglo-Saxon Chronicle for 755 plainly shows that Hittite *tas* and the Indo-European pronominal *so/to* come from a single source. That this source must be nearer to the analytic Hittite than to unanalyzable Indo-European is obvious.[11]

234. It remains to trace the development from the Proto-Indo-Hittite system to the one that must be assumed for Proto-Indo-European.

In Proto-Indo-Hittite there were three sentence connectives *to, so,* and *nu,* of which the first two were frequently combined with the enclitic pronoun *-os.* The third of these survives in the Indo-European languages as Sanskrit *nu,* Greek *ny,* Gothic *nu,* etc. The word clearly means 'now,' with shifts to 'surely, therefore, certainly' and the like.

We have written the second connective *so* on the assumption that it is the source of Greek *ho,* Sanskrit *sa,* and Gothic *sa,* nominative singular masculine of the stem *to-*. If we may assume that its original use was to introduce a sentence which recorded an action of the person who had been acting previously, it is easy to see how it was reinterpreted as a nominative singular. The change of the vowel to *u* in Hittite must be ascribed to the influence of the commonest of all the sentence connectives in that language, namely *nu.* If we may assume for the first connective, *to,* such a meaning as 'then, next' and may further assume that it was distinguished from *so* in being used when there was a new subject, the development of the Indo-European system is clear. In case there was no new subject, *so* was regularly employed; it came to be understood as the subject of the new verb. In case there was a new subject, *to* was employed alongside of the subject; it could not be reinterpreted as subject. Frequently it was accompanied by the accusative of the enclitic pronoun (yielding Indo-European *tom, tod, tons, ta*). In all probability the feminine did not exist in Proto-Indo-Hittite, but of course the feminine forms of the Indo-European *to*-pronoun were readily supplied by analogical creation. Analogical creation must also have filled in the oblique cases of the Indo-European *to*-stem. Hittite presents a few forms like *ta-si* 'et ei' (Proto-Indo-Hittite *to-soi*), which may well have served as models. No wonder, then, that the Proto-

11. I have posed in Language, 15. 15, a number of questions that must be answered by scholars who take the other view of the case.

Indo-European pronominal declension differs from the nominal declension!

There are other reasons for believing that Hittite and Proto-Indo-European are both descended from an earlier language that may be called Proto-Indo-Hittite, but this one reason is strong enough to establish the proposition.

235. No less than five other ancient languages of Asia Minor go rather closely with Hittite; Luwian and Palaic are known from citations in the Hittite documents; Lycian and Lydian from inscriptions of Greek times; and another language, commonly called Hieroglyphic Hittite, is known from inscriptions scattered over most of Asia Minor and northern Syria, datable from the middle of the second millennium to the middle of the first, B.C.[12] Together these languages constitute the Anatolian branch of the Indo-Hittite family. So little is known of most of them that the construction of a family tree is dangerous; the following scheme avoids all details.

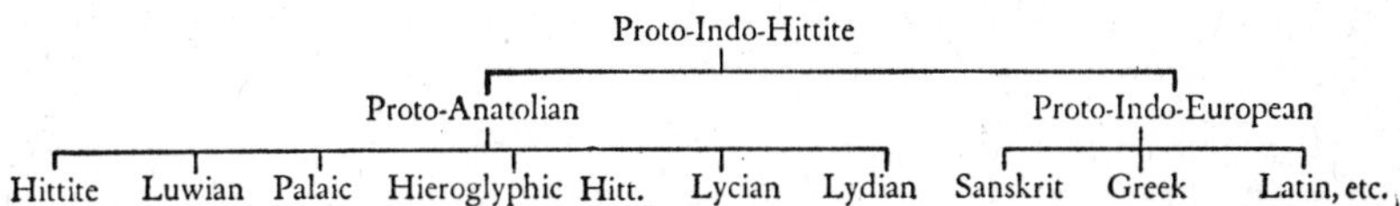

Figure 8.

The Anatolian languages preserve certain phonemes that have been lost in all the Indo-European tongues. The one for which the evidence is clearest is *x* (with approximately the sound in German *ach*), which appears, for example, in Hittite *xuxas,* Hieroglyphic Hittite *xuxas,* and Lycian *xugas* beside Latin *avus* 'grandfather.' We must reconstruct Proto-Indo-European *awos,* Proto-Anatolian *xuxas* or *xuxos,* Proto-Indo-Hittite *xauxos*. Another example of Hittite *x* is *xants* 'front,' dative singular *xanti* 'in front,' beside Sanskrit and Greek *anti,* Latin *ante* 'opposite.'

236. The comparative method has been applied thoroughly to the

12. For Luwian and Palaic, see Helmuth Th. Bossert, Ein hethitisches Königssiegel, pp. 77–132 (1944). For Hieroglyphic Hittite, see Ignace J. Gelb, Hittite Hieroglyphs III (1942), Elements of Hieroglyphic Hittite, Chicago (1947). For Lycian, see Holger Pedersen, Lykisch und Hittitisch (1945). For Lydian, see Piero Meriggi, Festschrift für Herman Hirt, pp. 283–290 (1936).

reconstruction of Proto-Indo-European, Proto-Romance (often called Vulgar Latin), Proto-Germanic, Proto-Celtic, and Proto-Slavic.[13] Somewhat less thorough use of the method has been made in reconstructing Proto-Semitic, Proto-Finno-Ugrian, and Proto-Bantu. Work has been well begun on the Malayo-Polynesian languages, Algonquian, and several other groups. There remain to be worked over all the other language groups of the world. Everywhere the task is extremely laborious, but everywhere the harvest is rich.

237. We pointed out early in this chapter that the comparative method can be applied only to related languages that have undergone a long separate development; borrowed features must be eliminated as rigorously as a judge excludes hearsay from the evidence taken in a court of law. This requirement, however, is difficult to apply. If two communities speaking related languages are separated by mountains or seas or by speakers of other languages, the chances are good for the success of the comparative method; but there is the chance that the present separation is of late date. Perhaps the two communities lived in immediate contact until so recently that their independent linguistic development has been negligible. An attempt to reconstruct an earlier phase of English by comparing the present speech of London and of Australia would certainly fail.

On the other hand, communities speaking closely related dialects and living in immediate contact are sure to show the effects of borrowing in proportion to the intensity of the intercommunication. This has always been the case throughout the western continental region of the Roman Empire, the countries of France, Spain, Portugal, and Italy. Hugo Schuchardt[14] has left an account of an imaginary journey on foot through northwestern Italy in the attempt to find the Italian-French linguistic boundary; the outcome is that there is no one boundary, but a great many isoglosses (**§ 50**). Since there has always been intercommunication, the dialects everywhere overlap. One might be inclined to conclude that

13. See especially Karl Brugmann, Grundriss der vergleichenden Grammatik der indogermanischen Sprachen, 2d ed. 2 vols. in 5, Strassburg (1897–1916); Kurze vergleichende Grammatik der indogermanischen Sprachen, Strassburg (1904); Meyer-Lübke, Grammatik der romanischen Sprachen, 3 vols., Leipzig (1890–1902); Holger Pedersen, Vergleichende Grammatik der keltischen Sprachen, 2 vols., Göttingen (1909–13); Antoine Meillet, Le slave commun, Paris (1934).

14. Hugo Schuchardt, Über die Klassifikation der romanischen Mundarten = Hugo Schuchardt-Brevier, pp. 144–166.

the comparison of Italian, Provençal, Spanish, Portuguese, and French would be quite futile, and that the reconstruction of Vulgar Latin would have to be based upon a comparison of continental Romance with the languages of the islands and with Rumanian.

238. This proves not to be the case. By carefully eliminating all sorts of borrowing, especially the "learned" loans from classical Latin, it has been possible to learn a great deal about Vulgar Latin by the comparison of the literary languages of Italy, Spain, and France, although Sardinia, Dalmatia, and Rumania have contributed a disproportionate amount. The reason is that after the collapse of the Roman Empire, at least until the end of the Middle Ages, communication over this area was largely confined to the upper classes. Even though the peasant could normally talk with his near neighbors, he had no need for more than that. Consequently linguistic innovations have spread very slowly, and distant points have remained relatively uninfluenced. It happened that the early comparatists had their attention fixed upon the literary languages, and these were based upon local dialects far enough apart to have been little influenced by one another after Roman times. Furthermore, scholars were no doubt helped by the possession of Latin texts which provided a ready check upon inferences from linguistic comparison. If anyone was inclined to stress the agreement of all the great literary languages, including Rumanian, upon a different treatment of Latin *c* before *ē̆* and *ī̆* and before other vowels, he was immediately confronted by Latin *cīvis, cinis, cēpī,* and *cedō* with the same initial consonants as *capiō, causa, cōdex, cupidus,* etc. Although the conditions prevailing throughout western Romania favor the use of the method of linguistic geography, the application of the comparative method to the documents of the literary languages has yielded useful results.

The earlier Romance comparatists depended chiefly upon early texts, and neglected local dialects completely, since they had no information about them. The publication of the linguistic atlases of France, Italy, and Catalonia (§§ 51–53) supplied abundant information about local dialects and made it possible to correct and supplement the conclusions of the comparatists at many points. The enthusiasm for this new material and the abundant detail of linguistic history that it disclosed has led some Romance scholars to undervalue the work of their predecessors. They have failed to recognize the fairly sharp division that exists between comparative grammar and the study of linguistic geography. It is nevertheless true that the opportunity for sound work in comparative grammar begins precisely at the point where there is evidence of a period of independent linguistic development in two or more communities. The line is not easy to draw; it is perhaps the outstanding problem still faced by linguistic science.

239. Far more difficult than in the Romance field is it to determine which common features of early Indo-European languages may or must be regarded as loans. Undoubtedly there was more or less dialectic division within the linguistic community that spoke Proto-Indo-European before the migrations began to carry Indo-European speech over a large part of the Eastern Continent. There is no reason why these dialectic differences should not survive in the historical languages, much as the dialectic peculiarities of English speech reappear in present-day American (§ 217).

No one has found a clear answer to this problem as yet, but one may protest against the easy assumption in some quarters that almost any linguistic feature common to two or more early Indo-European languages may, without more ado, be ascribed to a Proto-Indo-European dialect. Thus, the widespread change of *s* > *h* is listed [15] as one of the "recent southeastern innovations" of Proto-Indo-European, appearing in "Greek, Lycian, Albanian [in part], Phrygian . . . , Armenian, Iranian." This claim ignores the very close connection of the earliest Indic and Iranian texts; they are so similar that one may sometimes translate from one language into the other without harm to the metrical structure of verse. And yet Indic retains prevocalic *s* unchanged; are we to assume that in the community that developed the early hymns there were two inherited dialects, one of which retained prevocalic *s* while the other had lost it?

At present I merely want to point out that in two of the other languages listed above the change is demonstrably later than the separation of the Proto-Indo-European community. In the more conservative Lycian dialect we actually meet *s* in a number of words in which the less conservative dialect shows *h*.[16] As to Greek we have already seen (§ 32. 5

15. G. Bonfante and I. J. Gelb, The Position of "Hieroglyphic Hittite" among Indo-European Languages = Journal of the American Oriental Society, 64. 185, 187 f. (1944).

16. See Holger Pedersen, Lykisch und Hittitisch, p. 14, Copenhagen (1945).

and n. 7) that the Semitic character *cheth* [x], not *he* [h], was borrowed to represent original *s* initial and intervocalic; at that time the change of *s* > *h* was still incomplete. This change certainly took place in several early Indo-European languages independently.

The same may be true of other changes common to the earliest recorded form of two or more Indo-European languages. Nonetheless, Johannes Schmidt found too many correspondences between neighboring languages for them all to be ascribed to chance. We must admit the existence of dialectic differences within Proto-Indo-European. At present we cannot do very much about such features; but it is important to recognize their existence. In theory, at least, a period of dialectic differentiation preceded the final separation of the Indo-European languages from the parent stock.

INDEX

References are to section numbers.

R

S